SALES FORECASTING

CASSELL MANAGEMENT STUDIES

Advisory Editor: Albert Battersby, M.A., B.SC., F.R.I.C.

ESSENTIAL ACCOUNTING FOR MANAGERS by A. P. Robson
THE LAW AND THE BUSINESS MANAGER by A. Harding Boulton
SALES FORECASTING by Albert Battersby

Titles in preparation include:
CHOOSING AND USING OFFICE EQUIPMENT by S. J. Cordell
ANALYSING AND CONTROLLING BUSINESS PROCEDURES by J. O'Shaughnessy
THE EFFECTIVE USE OF COMPUTERS IN BUSINESS by Pat Losty
THE MULTINATIONAL FIRM by David T. Frost
TRAINING FOR TRAINING OFFICERS by S. E. Godfrey
NETWORK ANALYSIS IN PROJECT MANAGEMENT by K. G. McLaren and
E. L. Buesnel

BY THE SAME AUTHOR

A Guide to Stock Control (B.I.M./Pitman, 1962)
Network Analysis for Planning and Scheduling (Macmillan, 2nd edn 1967)
Mathematics in Management (Penguin, 1966)

SALES
FORECASTING

ALBERT BATTERSBY

CASSELL · LONDON

CASSELL & COMPANY LTD
35 Red Lion Square, London WC1

Melbourne, Sydney, Toronto,
Johannesburg, Auckland

© Albert Battersby 1968

First published 1968

S.B.N. 304 92330 3

*Printed offset in Great Britain by
The Camelot Press Ltd,
London and Southampton*

F.168

. . . a notable example of the mad and fond curiositie of our nature, ammusing it selfe to preoccupate future things, as if it had not enough to doe to digest the present.

MONTAIGNE, *Of Prognostications*

First I'll instruct thee in the rudiments
And then wilt thou be perfecter than I.

MARLOWE, *Doctor Faustus*

CONTENTS

1 General Considerations   1

2 Moving Averages   21

3 Weighted Moving Averages   43

4 Regression Analysis   54

5 Seasonal Effects   80

6 Market Saturation   91

Appendix: Logarithms   103

Solutions to Exercises   119

References   139

Index   141

ACKNOWLEDGEMENTS

At the time this book reached the proof stage, I was convalescing from a serious illness and Eric Duckworth came to my aid by reading the proofs; this he did with great thoroughness, relieving me of a considerable mental load while at the same time offering mild but informed criticism of the text. This latter has been acted on to the improvement of the book, but does not make Mr Duckworth in any way responsible for its contents: the subjective judgements which creep in here and there are mine alone. I must also thank Cassell's staff for their patience, understanding and skilled and sympathetic help.

Mr A. C. Nielsen Senr provided the data for Fig. 4.12 and, with his company, gave permission for its use. I must also thank the Editors of *Work Study and Management* and the *Operational Research Quarterly* for permission to use material originally published by them and on which are based the case studies in Chapters 5 and 6 respectively.

Sales executives who have attended my seminars at the British Institute of Management and the College of Marketing have contributed much to this book by their frank interchange of experience and their constructive criticism.

I have also drawn on experience gained in sales forecasting, stock control and studies of distribution for the British Petroleum Company and am grateful to that company for permission to do so.

Finally, I thank Miss Ann Smith who typed the first drafts, my wife who helped me shape them into the finished MS. and, as ever, Johnnie Johnson and his staff at Cranfield for help with the diagrams. How pleasant it is to live in a world where everyone is so helpful!

ALBERT BATTERSBY

INTRODUCTION

Cassell Management Studies

Management is, and must always remain a practical subject, and all the books in the Cassell Management Studies series are addressed to the practical man. Among these practical managers are several who within the last century, roughly, have tried to systematize their knowledge of management practice, to classify it, and sometimes to derive laws from it. For example we can take Taylor, who, working sixty or seventy years ago, first of all found out what it was reasonable to expect a machine to do: how fast one could expect it to produce work under specified conditions. Taylor then went on to similar studies on the human being. More recently this study of the individual human being has opened out into studies of groups of human beings who form themselves into organizations, and much of modern management research has been directed at this study of organizations, how they are formed, how they *should* be formed, what their goals are and so on, and the study of organization is one of the sub-headings of management studies in general. We can think of others, for example, Marketing and Accounting, and the books to be published in this series will eventually cover the whole gamut of sub-sections of management as a whole.

The books themselves will be diverse in their treatment of the subject. Some, for example, will be designed as textbooks, others as original contributions in fields where research is scattered over professional journals and where collected works are scarce or non-existent. A more important sub-section of the series will be books on specialized aspects of management designed to give the practising manager or the aspiring manager an overall view of the subject as a whole. Many books of this type will be contained in the first issues in the series. For example, the very first book to be published, already successful, is one on Accounting by Robson. This excellent little summary will give the manager a good send-off in the study of the amount of accounting he, as a manager, needs to know about.

This is followed by a similar book on Law, not a treatise on law, but a survey designed to show the manager what aspects of the law are relevant to his job, to give him an outline of what the law says about these aspects, and to suggest to him when he has reached the point at which he should go for further advice to a lawyer. After this will come similar books on computers, on organization and on such subjects as work study. Each book will be written by a specialist in the relevant field, but the aim will always be to give a readable account of the subject treated.

We hope that readers of these books will assist us by sending in criticisms either of individual books or of the series as a whole, and suggestions for other books, especially on areas which they feel are not at present served adequately by the published literature.

A. B.

1 GENERAL CONSIDERATIONS

The purpose of this book is to show sales managers some of the methods which may help them to improve their forecasts. It follows three main principles: first, that the presentation shall be non-mathematical, apart from elementary arithmetic and graphs; secondly, that the emphasis shall be on the simpler and more widely used procedures. The third principle, often overlooked, is that a critical approach is essential in selecting the most suitable method from the many which are available; the sales manager, who is the customer in this case, must not only have the methods displayed to him but needs to be advised of their appropriateness to his own needs. What is equally important, he must be told their limitations: a six-volt solution is useless to a man with a 230-volt problem, and vice versa.

This first chapter is a general survey of the main features which a forecaster should consider before he goes to work on the actual data.

The Economics of Forecasting

All forecasts are wrong. They differ in the extent of their wrongness, and it is usually possible to improve any forecast by gathering further relevant information or by processing, in a more elaborate way, what is already known. This costs money or time, the expenditure of which can only be justified if greater benefits ensue. Errors in forecasts have to be covered either by holding stocks, or by keeping production capacity 'in reserve' (which means idle) or by having emergency sources of supply. All these expedients cost money, and the art of good forecasting lies in getting the greatest savings at the lowest cost. One branch of this art—stock control—has been described in some detail elsewhere. [6]

The forecaster, then, aims to get the highest value out of his work, and not necessarily the greatest accuracy for its own sake. The spending of money (or time) is controlled by the *decisions* of the executive for whom the forecast is made, and the action which he subsequently takes. It is logical to look first at the process of decision-making since this defines the purpose of any *business* forecast (as distinct from a purely academic one).

Decisions

Every decision requires an estimate of its outcome and hence involves a forecast.

A forecast is an array of information which helps a manager to reach a decision. The nature of the decision defines the *purpose* of the forecast,

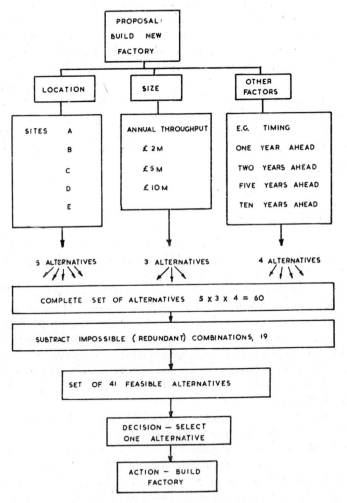

Figure 1.1 Structure of a decision

and it follows that no business forecast, whether mathematical or intuitive, can be independent of the decisions which flow from it.

A decision is a selection of some course of action from a set of alternatives; after the decision has been made, appropriate action is taken. A characteristic of action is that it is irreversible: it will cause the old set of alternatives to be replaced by a new one. The new set may differ only slightly from the previous set if the action was fairly trivial; it may be considerably altered if the action, and therefore the decision from which it stemmed, was a major one.

Figure 1.1 shows how this abstract concept of decision-making would apply to a particular decision: building a new factory. The complete set of alternatives is generated by considering the individual relevant factors—location, size, and so on—in all their possible combinations. Some of the combinations will not be feasible—for example, sites A, B and C may be too small for a factory with £10 m. a year throughput; site D may not be available until five years' time; the company's finances may not permit the largest size of factory to be built until after next year. Subtracting these redundant combinations leaves a set of feasible alternatives, as shown in Figure 1.2. This descrip-

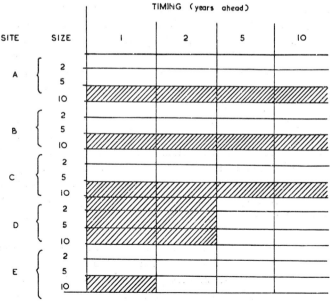

Figure 1.2 Feasible (white) and redundant (shaded) combinations of factors

tion is over-simplified—in practice the whole range of alternatives would gradually be whittled down by a series of decisions and actions rather than by a single all-embracing one—but the general principle which it illustrates is still valid.

Alongside this decision structure runs a forecasting structure. The final decision will be based on forecasts of the outcomes of each of the alternatives. The individual forecasts may be made with varying degrees of exactitude, and may include judgment and 'hunches' as well as measured factors. Thus, site E is in an overseas country and may be quickly discarded because of political instability. No one can measure political instability—it is a case for intuition.

We must not overlook the prior decision which initiated the whole subject; the decision to set up the investigation in the first place. It would itself be based on a forecast of a favourable trend in a particular market—and it is with forecasts of this type that the technical part of this book will mainly be concerned.

Tactics and Strategy

Decisions within a company may be grouped under two main headings. First come the **tactical** ones which govern day-to-day running, and which demand that short-term forecasts be produced as a matter of routine. They are concerned with the manipulation of a limited set of resources, as in working out the loading of machines, buying material for routine manufacture or planning the visits of a force of sales representatives.

Strategic decisions, on the other hand, determine the limits of the resources themselves: should more machine tools be installed? Can research discover new raw materials? Is the sales force of the right size? Should we enter new markets? Such problems extend over a longer span of time, involve bigger sums of money, and have a greater influence on the lives of the people they may affect. They generate a need for long-term forecasting.

There is an essential difference between the two types of decision. It centres upon their association with random disturbances and trends. A sales department operates in a market which imposes casual random disturbances upon it—customers place orders which, although expected, come in earlier or later than usual; new customers enter the market and old ones leave it; a representative falls ill; production machinery breaks down. The last two examples show that the market is not the *only* source of disturbances—the whole business environment of the sales department may produce them, and this includes other parts of the same company as well as its customers. **Tactical decisions** aim to nullify these disturbances so that the internal affairs of the business run smoothly. Decisions to draw from stock smooth out the production load in the face of fluctuating sales; overtime working may be sanctioned to counteract a breakdown in machinery; a retiring employee may be replaced in order to keep the work-force constant. These are all routine decisions.

The environment also generates **trends**—markets expand, social conditions change, technology advances. Far from opposing these trends and trying to nullify their effects, the business must adjust itself to them if it is to survive: it will do so through its strategic decisions. The detection of such trends and their separation from random fluctuations is therefore an important part of any forecasting procedure. A characteristic problem in separating trends from random effects is illustrated in Figure 1.3. Most observers, judging by eye, would

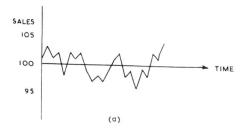

Figure 1.3 Trends and random fluctuations

agree that the sales graph in (*b*) shows only random variations, whereas that in (*c*) has a definite upward trend in the last few periods—but what about (*a*), which is the same as both (*b*) and (*c*) with only the last figure removed? If we had to forecast from (*a*) alone, should we say that sales were starting to show signs of an upward trend or not? Finding reasonable answers to such questions is vital to proper managerial decisions, and is an essential component of any forecasting method.

The Question of Scale

All decisions must be viewed in relation to the general scale of a company's operations. Thus, a decision to buy a new lorry may be routine to the Transport Manager of an industrial giant, the vehicle being acquired as extra insurance against the hazards of breakdown. To a small owner-operator, however, it could be a 50 per cent increase in his total resources, and the decision would be taken against a (to him) long-term view of his ability to employ it.

The Critical Approach

In forecasting, as in other spheres of management, it is all too easy to rush in with mathematical methods as

> The tools of working out salvation
> By mere mechanic operation.

When forecasting can be reduced to a purely mathematical routine, we can write the procedure down as equations, as a list of instructions for an electronic computer or for a human being (see the example on page 13). The formal statement may then be referred to as a **mathematical model**. Success in using a mathematical model can only come if the model represents the real world well enough for the purpose in hand. The purpose—decision leading to action—has already been settled.

Short-term and Long-term Forecasts

The short term and long term for forecasting are often defined arbitrarily by associating different periods of time with them. 'Short term' may mean anything from a day ahead to a year ahead. 'Long term' may extend from a year to as much as half a century; the General Post Office, for instance, looks forty years ahead.

It is more rational to associate these two expressions with the types of decisions to which they apply: to do so gives us the following definitions.

A **short-term forecast** is one which provides information for tactical decisions; it is therefore concerned with day-to-day operations *within the limits of the resources currently available*. It usually needs to be accompanied by estimates of the random fluctuations which the tactical decisions aim to reduce.

A **long-term forecast** is one which provides information for major strategic decisions: it is concerned with *extending or reducing the limits of the resources*. Its emphasis therefore tends to be mainly on trends. It follows that long-term decisions will mainly be about capital expenditure and short-term ones about revenue.

A medium-term forecast is similar to a long-term one, but it concerns minor strategic decisions which change the limits of resources to a relatively small extent.

Figure 1.4 shows a systematic critical approach to the development of a forecast, beginning with two main features—information and

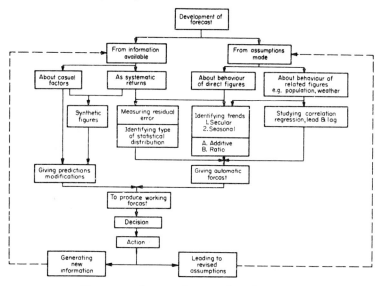

Figure 1.4 The critical approach to forecasting

assumptions. First we consider the behaviour of the direct figures; for a sales forecast, they will be the past records of the sales we are going to forecast, and are part of the systematic returns. The need for these figures is obvious: what is not so obvious is how the forward projection of them is affected by our *assumptions* about their behaviour. Such assumptions are rarely stated explicitly, but are carried somewhere in the back of the forecaster's mind; on them depend the rules which will make up the 'model', mathematical or otherwise, of our forecasting procedure. It is essential to identify them and bring them out into the open. If we do so, we shall be able to link our forecasting model more closely to reality by incorporating in it those influences which we believe to exist in the business world.

The Effects of Different Assumptions

We shall begin by taking a series of sales figures (Table 1.I) and seeing how different assumptions about their behaviour will affect forecasts developed from them.

TABLE 1.I

Monthly Sales of a Commodity, in Gallons

Month	Sales
January	271
February	262
March	253
April	245
May	114
June	165
July	108
August	189
September	287
October	339
November	325
December	442
Total for the year:	3,000
Monthly average	250

If we simply say that these sales are subject to random fluctuations and nothing else, then we imply that there are no systematic trends, so the best guide to future sales will be the average, 250 gallons a month.

The forecast sales for the next six months will then be $6 \times 250 = 1,500$ gallons.

Secular Trends

Now let us make a different assumption and set about identifying trends (see Figure 1.4). A **secular trend** is one which causes sales to go on increasing or decreasing indefinitely. In this case, we shall assume that an upward or downward trend exists, and do the following simple sum:

	Gallons
Sales in second six months	1,690
Sales in first six months	1,310
Difference over six months	+380

giving an increase of 63 gallons every month.

Since sales have increased by 380 gallons over two successive half-years, we would assume a corresponding increase in the next half-year. We must now decide whether the trend is **additive** (or **linear**), that is to say, that sales are increasing by a constant *quantity* each year, or **multiplicative** when they will increase by a constant **ratio**. In the latter case, the trend is said to be **exponential**.

If the trend is additive, the forecast for the next six months will be $1,690 + 380 = 2,070$ gallons. If it is exponential, we first calculate the ratio for the two periods; $1,690/1,310 = 1.29$, and apply this to obtain a forecast of $1,690 \times 1.29 = 2,180$ gallons. An alternative way of doing the latter calculation is to say that sales increase by 29 per cent every six months. Table 1.II gives a summary of the results.

TABLE 1.II

Effect of assumption on forecasts from sales figures in Table 1.I

Assumption	Forecast, gallons
No trend	1,500
Secular trend (additive)	2,070
Secular trend (ratio)	2,180

Thus we see how three different assumptions give three different forecasts.

Exercise 1.1

The number of inquiries received at the London Weather Centre was 98,600 in 1958 and 114,000 in 1959. Forecast the number of inquiries in 1960, assuming

(*a*) that the number of inquiries is subject only to random fluctuations but has no upward or downward trend;

(*b*) that any random fluctuations are negligibly small, but that there is a constant additive increase every year.

(*c*) As (*b*), except that the increase is exponential (multiplicative).

Exercise 1.2

The actual number of inquiries received in 1960 was 178,000. If you now wish to forecast the figure for 1961, which assumption would you favour—(*a*), (*b*), (*c*) or some other one?

Seasonal Trends

Sales and other figures will sometimes show a regular, rhythmical variation upwards and downwards, constituting a **seasonal trend**. By their very nature, seasonal trends do not affect the general level, and will always tend to cancel out in the long run. The rhythm of variation is usually an annual one, but trade cycles and other phenomena may have an effect over longer or shorter periods; for example, spending on entertainment follows a weekly pattern, being heaviest at the end of the week. A popular theory in the 1930s even went so far as to relate business conditions to the eleven-year cycle of sunspot activity.

Professor Forrester of M.I.T., in his studies of 'Industrial Dynamics', has shown how misleading it may be to assume that 'seasonal' effects are necessarily caused by conditions *outside* the business, since they may be generated or aggravated by its own internal workings. In seeking seasonal effects, especially yearly ones, we are usually led to look beyond the figures themselves to a prime cause such as annual variations in temperature or hours of daylight, or recurrences of feasts like Easter and Christmas. A closer study of the figures in Table 1.I might well lead to enquiries about possible sources of seasonal effects. Table 1.III shows one approach.

TABLE 1.III

Quarterly Totals and Averages from Table 1.I

Sales, gallons

	Total for quarter	Average per month
First Quarter	786	262
Second Quarter	524	175
Third Quarter	584	195
Fourth Quarter	1,106	369

This analysis gives reason to suspect a seasonal effect which causes sales to rise in winter and fall in summer.

Exercise 1.3

You are now told that the figures in Table 1.I are for sales of:
(a) heating oil;
(b) ice cream.
Does this extra information affect your assessment of whether or not a seasonal trend exists?

The simple example in Exercise 1.3 shows how additional information can help us to decide on the most appropriate type of forecasting model. Generally speaking, the greater the amount of relevant information included, the better will be the forecast. For example, if you were now to be told that Table 1.I was for sales in Melbourne, your assessment of seasonal influences would certainly alter.

Related Figures

In detecting and measuring trends we are not necessarily limited to considering only the direct figures. Many businesses study the behaviour of related figures for use in their own forecasting (see Figure 1.4). The gas and electricity boards use short-term weather forecasts in predicting their own sales: so do ice cream manufacturers and distributors of fuel. One gramophone record company uses sales of gramophones as a guide to the demand for records (see Figure 1.6, 'phonograph correlation', although 'regression' would be the better term—see below). Industries use each others' forecasts in deriving their own. Thus, forward estimates for the production of steel, coal, cement, alkali and sulphuric acid are often taken as general predictors of a country's overall economic progress. Population increase is of obvious importance to manufacturers of consumer goods, and so are economic plans such as a rational target for the annual increase in economic activity.

Related figures may be used vaguely as an aid to 'hunch' predictions, but the methods of mathematical statistics include means of *measuring* the extent to which two variables are related. They include **correlation** and **regression analysis**. Broadly speaking, correlation measures the relationship between two variables without necessarily implying that either is the *cause* of the other. For example, an increase in the demand for bricks may be correlated with that for structural steel, the prime cause of both being more building. Regression analysis, on the other hand, is based on causal relationships, when there is good reason to believe that some factor *affects* sales. Examples from real life include:

(i) orders for cigarettes in a given area depend on whether or not a sales representative visits that area;

(ii) sales of soft drinks are affected by temperature;

(iii) sales of anti-freeze are affected by the incidence of the *first* autumn frost.

Changes in one variable do not necessarily have an immediate effect on the other: one may **lead** and the other **lag**. An increase in the number of motor-cars sold causes the demand for steel to rise but only after a lag of about eighteen months; the output figures for cars therefore provide a useful predictor of subsequent activity in the steel industry. Shorter lead-and-lag times are known: one company making photographic goods has found that when processed colour films are returned to photographers, a certain proportion of queries arises. These arrive a few weeks later as letters, and the load on the office which handles them can be predicted from the number of films processed in the preceding weeks.

Errors in Forecasts

No projection of past figures into the future will ever give a perfect forecast, except by a fluke. The **errors** in forecasts may be so small as to be negligible, but this is rare in business. Many crises and conflicts caused by such errors could be avoided if statistical methods were more widely used. Such methods allow the degree of error to be *measured* so that one can work out positive ways of dealing with uncertainty, instead of merely grumbling about it. It is worth pointing out that the word 'error' is used in a technical sense by statisticians: it means 'the magnitude of a random fluctuation' and does not imply any sort of 'wrongness' in the data.

These fluctuations are measured after all the systematic effects—the trends—have been corrected for. They are therefore called **residual error** (see Figure 1.4) and part of the statistician's approach to their measurement is in identifying the type of **statistical distribution** to which they conform. It is a remarkable fact that random errors, although individually unpredictable, tend to obey certain mathematical laws when they are looked at in groups: for instance, big errors are usually much rarer than small ones. The groups or 'families' of errors, and the laws which describe them, are what we mean when we talk about a 'statistical distribution'.

Automatic Forecasting

By identifying trends, studying correlations and measuring errors, we arrive at a set of mathematical rules which enable the sales manager to use blindly mechanical methods to get an automatic forecast. This work may be delegated to clerks who operate in complete ignorance of the market conditions but merely carry out the prescribed calculations. Alternatively (and more humanely) it may be done by an electronic computer.

Automatic forecasting can give surprisingly good results. Figure 1.5 shows a comparison of the errors made by a group of skilled executives in estimating the consumption of a commodity, and the errors made by an untrained clerk with a desk calculator, carrying out a quick mechanical routine. There is no great difference between the errors in the two cases; the clerk's results are, if anything, slightly better.

In general, though, completely automatic forecasting is not enough, as will be discussed later. Nevertheless, it can take much of the drudgery away from the sales manager by doing the routine projection of past figures—and doing it much better. He can then ignore all those products for which market conditions are not expected to change, and concentrate on the few more interesting ones: this is true 'management by exception'.

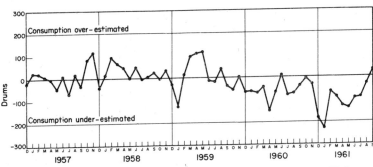

(*a*) Errors made by human forecasters. Mean = − 21·5   S.D. = 72·2

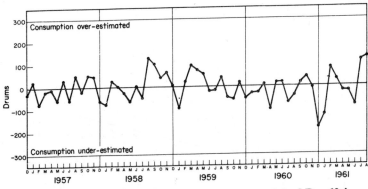

(*b*) Errors made by automatic forecasting. Mean = − 2·6   S.D. = 60·1

Figure 1.5

Comparison of errors

Data

The data used for forecasting will usually be one or more series of figures dealing with past performance, taken systematically at regular intervals, and known technically as **time series**. It is important to know how the figures were obtained and the purpose for which they are to be used. A common mistake, for example, is to confuse 'sales' with 'demand': using past sales figures as a forecast of future market capacity can sometimes be misleading. A sales manager dealing in canned foods for pets might know that people living in a poor area cannot afford to keep pets or, if they do, will feed them on scraps. He would go on to forecast a low demand and therefore make low deliveries to that area. People in these areas have been known to buy such foods for their own consumption, and this unconsidered factor might augment the demand. The sales cannot exceed the deliveries, so the *sales* would stay low in the face of a high unsatisfied demand. The manager concerned might then feel his original deduction to be correct, and continue to make low deliveries. He would also find his forecasts turning out to be remarkably accurate. (Whether he *ought* to make higher deliveries is a difficult ethical question beyond the modest scope of this book.)

If we interpret 'data' in the widest sense as embracing all the information which is relevant to a forecast, then we must also include casual facts—general market intelligence, gossip, news from the 'old-boy' network, non-quantitative reports from salesmen in the field, political rumours and so on. Such odd scraps of knowledge cannot be ignored, since they may drastically affect any aspect of a company's affairs: a rise of one per cent in the Bank Rate just before a debenture issue will change a forecast of cash flow; a cut in purchase tax will stimulate sales in the home market, and so on. R. G. Brown [1] has given the name of **prediction** to estimates based on this sort of information, reserving 'forecasting' for the automatic mathematical manipulation of systematic data. Here are his definitions:

Forecast the projection of the past into the future
Prediction management's anticipation of changes and of new factors affecting demand.

It would be generally true to say that, on the one hand, far more of the forecasting process is reducible to mechanical routines than most managers appreciate. On the other hand, the forecaster who ignores the predictive element supplied by the skill and experience of the manager and his staff, may be rejecting the most important single factor in any estimate of a future figure.

Synthetic Figures

One of the most important sources of market information can be found in the comments of a perceptive and enthusiastic sales force. They can feed back not only estimates of local market changes as systematic returns, but also describe the 'feel' of the market. Their rough quantitative estimates can be added up to give a total synthesis of the market, hence the name **synthetic figures** in Figure 1.4. Their judgments and 'hunches' can also be synthesized by the sales forecaster in his own 'predictive' contribution. Synthesis can also be built up from 'one-off' surveys of the market; although these are 'systematic' in that they are carefully planned and performed, they do not form a part of the regular business figures of a company. For example, the Royal MacBee company forecast the market for a new type of electric typewriter by a series of surveys: the figures obtained from them would be classified as synthetic in the scheme shown in Figure 1.4. [2]

Working Forecast

The end product of the procedure in Figure 1.4 is a **working forecast** on which the decision is based. This working forecast is obtained by first producing an automatic forecast—a projection of past data—using the routine methods to be described later. The automatic forecast may then be modified or even over-ridden by predictive factors, in much the same way as an airline pilot takes over from the automatic pilot when he suspects bad weather ahead.

A forecasting organization in an actual company, Capitol Records Inc. [3]—is shown diagrammatically in Figure 1.6, and many of the features of Figure 1.4 may be identified in it.

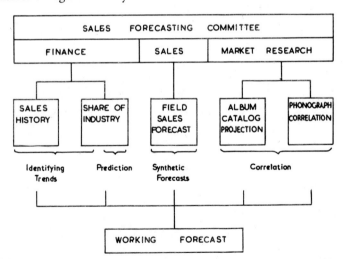

Figure 1.6 Organization and method of forecasting at Capitol Records Inc.

Closing the Loop

The final step in the critical approach to forecasting is 'closing the loop' as shown by the dotted lines in Figure 1.4. As soon as action is taken, it generates a new situation about which new information is fed back into the system. This information will affect future forecasts and may even change the current one. For example, if the working forecast indicates a fall in the demand for a product in a given area, the sales manager may well decide on a special sales drive in that area: then, through the 'casual factors–predictions' route in Figure 1.4, he will modify the previous forecast accordingly. His action will also affect the actual sales figures for the area, with a corresponding reaction on the next automatic forecast.

Two examples will serve to show how a forecast may initiate action which affects its own validity. The first is the American presidential elections for 1948, when opinion polls (forecasts based on sampling) showed a 4 per cent advantage for Dewey and foreshadowed an overwhelming defeat for Truman. The final poll in this series was made one month before the election, leaving time for change. Truman's consequent action was the 'whistle-stop' campaign, and he won the election. Although this case is often quoted as an argument against the reliability of opinion polls, it is equally arguable that, had the forecast not been made, and Truman remained passive, he would in fact have been defeated.

The second case is recovery from a slump, or 'business recession' as it is more euphemistically called. If, during a slump, a businessman predicts a recovery, he may start to expand his plant, re-equip with better machinery and build up stocks of material in anticipation. In doing so, he increases the volume of orders placed on other firms. A few optimistic men, acting in this way, can induce similar action in others, thus starting a flow of new orders and helping to initiate the recovery. It is for this reason that one of the main aims of the Chancellor of the Exchequer during a slump is to induce a general feeling of optimism about the future.

The closed loop also links up to the assumptions made. If a linear trend generates consistent underestimates, then a new assumption may be needed, which gives a more steeply ascending curve.

Figure 1.7 shows how this concept of a closed control loop may be applied to forecasting, and also gives a check list of some of the factors,

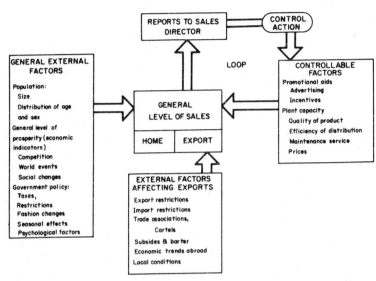

Figure 1.7 Factors in sales forecasting. (Based on material from *An Introduction to Business Forecasting*, p. 4. Institute of Cost and Works Accountants, London, 1960)

both internal and external, which may affect sales; it also suggests the actions which the sales director may take to follow the trend of sales (or to neutralize their random fluctuations).

Methods of Forecasting

When the critical examination of the purpose, assumptions, and data has been completed—and not before—we are free to select the method of forecasting. There are two main groups, synthetic and analytical.

Synthetic forecasts are built up from a number of individual reports, such as the returns from members of a large field sales force, and will not be considered in detail here. They have the advantages of using direct information and being easy to understand. Their disadvantages include individual bias, inadequate coverage and the lack of any estimate of their reliability; although based on numerical data, they contain a large element of prediction.

Analytical forecasts, conversely, break down total figures into trends and random elements which may be recombined to give a projection into the future. Since these methods are applied to time series, they are often grouped under the generic title of **time series analysis**. This genus of methods may be separated into species, of which regression analysis is predominant in business forecasting. A characteristic of time series in business is that they are **discrete**, being made up of figures taken at intervals rather than continuously, and regression analysis is particularly useful for investigating such series.

Analytical forecasting has two great advantages—it can be reduced to a routine and its error can be estimated: **confidence limits** may be calculated and suitable measures devised for dealing with the error. Its disadvantages are that because it is a routine, it may exclude relevant non-numerical facts, that it may be a complex and time-consuming procedure, and that the people called upon to use it may not clearly understand its mathematical aspects. The first of these may be overcome, as we have seen, by giving the predictor power to override the forecaster in reaching the final working forecast (Figure 1.4); electronic computers are the answer to the second, and education to the third.

The methods which will be introduced in the following pages range from very simple averaging procedures to the more elaborate forms of regression analysis. They are shown in Figure 1.8 arranged according

Increasing mathematical complexity →

	MOVING AVERAGES			REGRESSION ANALYSIS			
General methods	(a) With linear weighting (b) With exponential weighting (c) With other weightings (triangular, empirical, etc.)			(a) On untransformed data (b) On logarithms			
Detailed analysis	UNADJUSTED	WITH SECULAR TREND CORRECTION	WITH SECULAR & SEASONAL TREND CORRECTIONS	LINEAR	POLYNOMINAL	TRIG.	MULTIPLE
				ANALYSIS OF VARIANCE (Closely related to regression)			
Purpose	PROVIDE INDIRECT ESTIMATES OF ERRORS BY COMPARISON OF FORECAST AND ACTUAL			PROVIDE A DIRECT ESTIMATE OF ERRORS IN FORECAST (RESIDUALS)			
Procedure	UNAIDED HUMAN COMPUTATION ADEQUATE	UNAIDED HUMAN COMPUTATION POSSIBLE BUT EXPENSIVE; DESK CALCULATOR PREFERABLE; ELECTRONIC COMPUTER MAY BE JUSTIFIED					ELECTRONIC COMPUTER ESSENTIAL

Figure 1.8 Spectrum of methods of projection

to their complexity, into a rough 'spectrum' which will serve as a guide to the development of the book as a whole.

In general, the simpler methods are applied to short-term forecasts, where speed and cheapness must be considered. The more complex methods are used for long-term work, because the sums of money involved in strategic decisions are so much greater as to justify the long and expensive calculations. The picture is changing, however, as the use of electronic computers expands, in that they make it possible to apply even more complicated mathematics as a matter of routine.

2 MOVING AVERAGES

Averaging and Smoothing

The simplest method of sales forecasting is to say 'We shall sell in the next period exactly as much as we sell in the present one.' In other words, we begin by assuming sales to be at an absolutely constant level and our data consists of one single figure—sales in the immediately past period. Our assumption, like our data, is unlikely to be adequate and the actual figure will turn out to be different from the forecast one. At this point we add another assumption—that sales vary in an unpredictable way about some constant or **base level**; it is reasonable to extend this assumption by saying that the random errors have the same magnitude in both the present period and the one after, but act so as to cancel each other. So if our sales were 98 in the first period and we now find them to be 102 in the second, we say

	Actual Sales	=	Base Level of Sales	+	Random Error	
	98	=	100		−2	Case
	102	=	100		+2	A
Total	200	=	200		0	
Average	100					

A suitable base level is easily found: it is the average of the two figures. When we obtain the actual sales for a third period, say 88, we again average and get

	Actual Sales	=	Base Level of Sales	+	Random Error	
	98	=	96		+2	
	102	=	96		+6	Case
	88	=	96		−8	B
Total	288	=	288		0	
Average	96					

You might argue that the total error in Case A is 4 (i.e. 2+2) and 16 in Case B (2+6+8), but in many ways it is more convenient to deal with what is called the **algebraic sum**; this takes account of the plus and minus signs in front of each figure. The algebraic sum of the random errors is zero and always must be so when they are measured from the average.

C

We feel intuitively that this process brings us nearer and nearer to some 'true' value of the base level of sales, as more figures are added into the average: this is called **smoothing** and implies that we are reducing the fragment of random error which still remains in the average.

Suppose that by some gift of clairvoyance we discovered that the true base level of sales really was 97, and had always been so. Then in Case A, our *estimate* of the base level (100) obtained by averaging, would differ from the true level (97) by an error of $+3$. In Case B, the error of the estimate would be -1. In real life, we hardly ever know the 'true' base level and are forced to deal only with estimates of it.

Exercise 2.1

Assume that each figure in Table 1.I (page 8) is made up from a base level and a random error. Estimate the base level. Calculate the random errors and find their total (algebraic sum).

If we stick rigidly to the assumption that the sales are made up of a true base level plus a random element, it follows logically that the greater the number of sales figures we incorporate into our average, the better it will be as an estimate of the true base level—the so-called 'law of averages'. Yet no one in his senses would go on accumulating figures into an average over an indefinite period. Why not? Because if he were to do so, and the base level *did* begin to change, the average would be very slow in responding.

Once we have admitted the possibility of such a change, we have added another assumption: that the base level is *not* constant but may show a **trend**. For the sake of making our average responsive to any trend that may appear, we discard some of the older figures as new ones come in, keeping a constant number of figures from which our working average is calculated. It then becomes a moving average.

Moving Averages

The **moving average** is one of the simplest forecasting methods available: one assumes that a slight trend upwards or downwards may exist, but will be negligibly small over the period covered by the forecast when compared with the random errors. The number of periods over which the moving average is calculated is often chosen so that it covers a whole year, giving a **moving annual average** (MAA). The MAA of the figures in Table 1.I is 250. If the figure for January of the following year turned out to be 422, the new moving average would be one-twelfth of the new total taken over the period from February to January. The easiest way of computing it is to subtract the old January figure from the new January figure and add one-twelfth of this difference to the old MAA.

$$\text{Adjustment} = \frac{422 - 271}{12} = 13$$

$$\text{New MAA} = 250 + 13 = 263$$

Exercise 2.2

Continuing Table 1.I, new figures for February and March are 381 and 394. Calculate the new moving averages, rounded to the nearest whole number.

An alternative method of revising a moving average is to work from the **moving totals**, as this reduces the rounding error caused by adjusting each average to the nearest whole number. The adjustment for January would then be:

Old Moving Annual Total (MAT) =		3,000
Adjustment = 422 − 271	=	+ 151
		―――
New MAT	=	3,151
Divide by 12 to obtain new MAA =		263

Exercise 2.3

Repeat the calculations of Exercise 2.2 but adjusting the MAT's instead of the MAA's.

Note about Rounding off

How should we round off a figure like 100·5, which is exactly between two whole numbers? Many people round off to the next highest whole number, 101 in this instance (Method B *overleaf*). A better rule is to round off to the nearest *even* number (Method A), as the following figures demonstrate.

Unrounded figures	Rounded by Method A	Rounded by Method B
4	4	4
1·5	2	2
3·5	4	4
2	2	2
2·5	2	3
0·5	0	1
1	1	1
3	3	3
Sum 18	18	20

Although these figures were chosen so as to exaggerate the difference between the two methods, it is nevertheless generally true that Method B will tend to give rounded figures which are on the whole too high.

Exercise 2.4

Calculate Moving Annual Totals and Averages for the following series of sales figures (to the nearest whole number).

Month	Sales	Sales in same month of preceding year	Total	Average
—	—	—	1,201	100
J	99	101	1,199	
F	101	103		
M	102	101		
A	98	102		
M	99	98		
J	96	102		
J	99	101		
A	98	102		
S	102	99		
O	101	97		
N	104	98		
D		97		
Annual Total		1,201		

The figures given in Exercise 2.4 and its solution are in fact those for which Figure 1.3 (a) is the graph. The smoothing effect of the moving average can be clearly seen in the solution.

Exercise 2.5

Forecast the sales for December in Exercise 2.4.

Exercise 2.6

Forecast the sales for the whole of the following year, from the data in Exercise 2.4.

The Effect of a Secular Trend

In selecting a moving average as a method of forecasting, we assume that the secular trend is negligibly small. What happens if we cannot make such an assumption? This may be seen most easily by looking at a series which is free from random error, but develops an additive trend and then becomes steady at a new level: see Table 2.I. Both the table and its graph in Figure 2.1 show how the moving average takes several periods to settle down to a rate of increase equal to that of the original sales figures and, later, to stabilize at the new higher level. When it *has* settled down to increase steadily, it still lags behind the actual sales, and the amount by which it lags is discussed below.

Note that the dotted line showing the actual sales in Fig. 2.1 is a straight line, and this will always be so when the trend is *constant* and *additive*. For this reason, mathematicians call such a trend **rectilinear** or, more commonly, just **linear**.

Figure 2.2 shows the relationship between the **time-lag** and the **time-span** or number of periods over which the moving average is taken. The average is, strictly speaking, a figure which corresponds to the middle of the span of time over which it is taken, and the time-lag is approximately half this span. More precisely,

$$\text{Time-Lag} = \tfrac{1}{2}\,(\text{Time-span} - 1),$$

both the time-lag and the time-span being expressed in sales periods. Some economists prefer to tabulate the moving average alongside the period in the middle of the span, in which case they would move up the second column of Table 2.I by two rows so that the first figure 100 would be opposite period 3. The third column would be moved up by one row. In this way, for example, all the 150s would be equal at period 10.

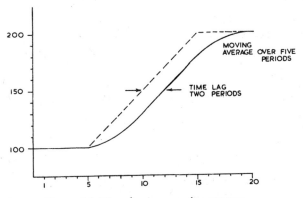

Figure 2.1 Time-lag in a moving average

TABLE 2.1

Time lag in a Moving Average

		Moving Averages	
Period	Sales	Over 5 periods	Over 3 periods
1	100		
2	100		
3	100		100
4	100		100
5	100	100	100
6	110	102	103
7	120	106	110
8	130	112	120
9	140	120	130
10	150	130	140
11	160	140	150
12	170	150	160
13	180	160	170
14	190	170	180
15	200	180	190
16	200	188	197
17	200	194	200
18	200	198	200
19	200	200	200
20	200	200	200

(Dotted lines show time-lags of two periods and one
period respectively.)

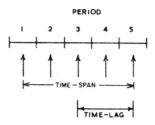

Figure 2.2 Time-lag in discrete periods

Exercise 2.7

Find the lag of the moving average over 3 periods in Table 2.I by using the rule given above. Check by comparing it with the 'Sales' column in Table 2.I; and by drawing a rough diagram similar to Figure 2.2.

Exercise 2.8

What time-lag would you expect in a MAA calculated over 12 sales periods of 1 month each?

Exercise 2.9

Calculate moving annual totals and averages for the following series of sales figures (to the nearest whole number).

Month	Sales	Sales in same month of previous year	Moving Annual Total	Moving Annual Average
—	—	—	852	71
J	84	60		
F	86	62		
M	88	64		
A	90	66		
M	92	68		
J	94	70		
J	96	72		
A	98	74		
S	100	76		
O	102	78		
N	104	80		
D	106	82		
Annual total		852		

Exercise 2.10

Suppose that, instead of behaving as in Table 2.I, the sales jumped suddenly from 100 in period 5 to 200 in period 6 and remained at that level until period 12. Draw a graph corresponding to Figure 2.1 but showing the actual sales as a dotted line and the moving average over five periods as a solid line.

Lag versus Smoothing

The greater the number of periods over which a moving average is taken, the greater is its time-lag, which is a disadvantage. When a

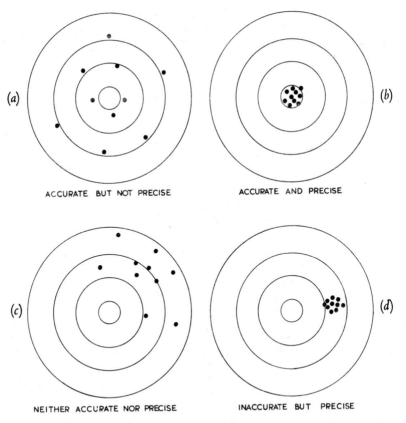

(a) ACCURATE BUT NOT PRECISE

(b) ACCURATE AND PRECISE

(c) NEITHER ACCURATE NOR PRECISE

(d) INACCURATE BUT PRECISE

Figure 2.3 Precision and accuracy

simple moving average is used to forecast sales which are showing an upward secular trend, it will lag behind and give *consistently* low estimates (or high ones if sales are falling). Any forecast which is consistently wrong is said to have **bias**, and the lower the bias, the more **accurate** is the forecast.

After any bias has been allowed for, the forecast will still have some element of random error in it. If the random error is small, the forecast is said to be **precise**. The words accurate and precise are used here in a technical sense, and are not interchangeable as in ordinary speech.

Figure 2.3 shows this in terms of shots at a target, and any marksman will see that accuracy and precision depend on different causes. Imprecise shooting may be due to inadequate training or to a worn barrel, whereas inaccurate shooting is more probably due to a bent foresight or a strong wind. Lack of accuracy may be corrected by 'aiming-off' and a moving average may also be adjusted in a similar way. The equivalent of aiming-off is to apply a **trend correction** as described later.

Exercise 2.11

If the 3-year moving averages in Table 2.I were used as forecasts, would they be (*a*) more accurate, (*b*) more precise than the 5-year averages?

The Precision of a Forecast

We have already seen that the **precision** of a forecast is some measure of its random error—but how are we to measure it? The average of the errors is a measure of the accuracy (or bias) of a forecast, and even when the bias is zero, the precision can still vary very greatly (see Figure 2.3a). We could take the difference between the highest and lowest errors as a measure of precision, but this would mean that we were discarding all the valuable information in the other figures. Our measure could also be distorted by a single freak error.

Statisticians have shown that a useful measure of precision may be obtained by averaging not the errors, but their squares. This gives what is known as the **variance**. A more convenient measure still is obtained if we 'unsquare' the variance, that is, take its square root. The result is then called the **standard deviation**, and this measure will frequently be referred to throughout this book.

(For technical reasons which will not be gone into here, the 'average' of the squared errors is obtained by dividing the total, not by the number of figures which make it up, but by one less than this number.)

Table 2.II shows some calculations which will serve to clarify the idea of a standard deviation. In each of the three series (a), (b) and (c), the errors are measured about the average rather than as differences from a forecast, but the principle remains the same.

TABLE 2.II

Standard Deviation as a Measure of Precision

	(a)	(b)	(c)
Data	100	100	100
	100	87	125
	100	112	90
	100	94	73
	100	107	112
	—	—	—
Total	500	500	500
Average	**100**	**100**	**100**
Errors	0	0	0
	0	−13	+25
	0	+12	−10
	0	−6	−27
	0	+7	+12
	—	—	—
Total	0	0	0
Sum of Squares of Errors	0	398	1,598
Variance	0	100	400
	—	—	—
Standard Deviation	**0**	**10**	**20**

The figures in series (a) have no deviation about the average at all: their standard deviation is zero; they resemble five shots making a single hole in the target and we may say that they are perfectly precise estimates.

Series (b) and (c) both vary about the average, and it is easy to see that (b) varies less than (c). By our measure, the standard deviation, (b) varies only half as much as (c) and is correspondingly more precise.

Exercise 2.12

The figures from which graph (a) in Figure 1.3 was drawn were:

101	103	101	102	98	102
101	102	99	97	98	97
99	101	102	98	99	96
99	98	102	101	104	

Their average is exactly 100; calculate their standard deviation.

Confidence Limits

Although there is no guarantee that the variability of any time series will remain constant, experience has shown that it rarely undergoes sudden changes in series of business returns. We may therefore assume the standard deviation to be constant and this enables us to predict not only the most probable value of the next figure in the series, but also the limits within which we can confidently assert that it will lie. For the sake of simplicity at this stage we shall assume that there is no trend, so no adjustment is needed.

One approximate rule is that in nineteen cases out of twenty, the next figure will be within two standard deviations of the average. There are many qualifications of this rule and extensions to it, but we shall use it as it stands to define the approximate confidence limits of any forecast, referring the more demanding reader to one of the standard works on statistics. [4] A limit of two standard deviations is often called a **two-sigma limit**.

Taking the three series in Table 2.II, our best estimate of the next figure to turn up would be 100 in each case, but the confidence limits would be

Series (a) 100± 0 i.e.   100
Series (b) 100±20 i.e. 80 to 120
Series (c) 100±40 i.e. 60 to 140

Confidence limits may be used to establish prudent safeguards against the random errors which cause an actual figure to differ from its forecast value. If the figures in Table 2.II represent the demands made on a production unit, and the manager plans to operate the unit at a steady rate of 100 items per period, it would be advisable for him to hold a stock, in cases (b) and (c). In the former, he might aim to begin each period within 20 items in hand, and in the latter with 40.

Exercise 2.13

We predict the next value for graph (*a*) in Figure 1.3 on the assumption that there is no trend. Our best prediction is therefore the average, 100.

(*a*) What confidence limits would you apply to this figure? (See Exercise 2.12.)

(*b*) Comment on the fact that the next figure as given by graph (*c*) is 107.

Estimating Secular Trends from Moving Averages

The difference between two successive moving averages gives an estimate of the secular trend between two periods, as shown by the following figures from Table 2.I.

Period	Sales	Moving Average over 5 periods	
5	100		
6	110		
7	120		
8	130		
9	140	120 ⎫ Difference	
10	150	130 ⎭ = +10	

If random errors are present, as they usually are, the estimate of the trend will contain some residual part of them. Nevertheless, it may be used to correct the time-lag.

In a 5-period moving average, the time-lag in the current period is *two* periods. If we want to forecast the next period ahead, we must apply a trend correction corresponding to *three* periods.

In the example just given, we should forecast sales for period 11 in the following way:

$$
\begin{aligned}
\text{Estimate of trend} &= +10 \text{ per period} \\
\text{Trend Correction for 3 periods} &= +30 \text{ (TC)} \\
\text{Current Moving Average} &= 130 \text{ (MA)} \\
\text{Forecast} = \text{MA} + \text{TC} &= 160
\end{aligned}
$$

Table 2.III and Figure 2.4 show that the method can give good results, in spite of an undershoot when the trend first develops and an overshoot when it flattens out. Note that trends and trend corrections have

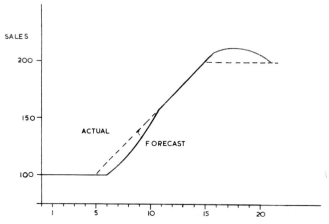

Figure 2.4 Moving average with trend correction used as forecast

TABLE 2.III

Moving Average over 5 periods with Trend Correction, used as Forecast

Period (0)	Sales (100)	MT	MA	Trend over one period	Trend Correction over three periods (TC)	Forecast = MA + TC
1	100					
2	100					
3	100					
4	100	500	100			
5	100	500	100	0	0	100
6	110	510	102	+2	+6	108
7	120	530	106	+4	+12	118
8	130	560	112	+6	+18	130
9	140	600	120	+8	+24	144
10	150	650	130	+10	+30	160
11	160	700	140	+10	+30	170
12	170	750	150	+10	+30	180
13	180	800	160	+10	+30	190
14	190	850	170	+10	+30	200
15	200	900	180	+10	+30	210
16	200	940	188	+8	+24	212
17	200	970	194	+6	+18	212
18	200	990	198	+4	+12	210
19	200	1,000	200	+2	+6	206
20	200	1,000	200	0	0	200

to carry plus or minus signs to show whether they are upwards or downwards.

Table 2.IV is an example of the trend-correction method applied to actual figures having a trend of unknown type and containing random fluctuations.

TABLE 2.IV

Forecasting Demand for Electricity

Year	Thousands of megawatt-hours	3-year MT	3-year MA	Trend	Forecast = 3-year MA + 2 × Trend	Error = Forecast – Actual
1956	6·826					
1957	7·125					
1958	7·724	21·675	7·225			
1959	8·245	23·094	7·698	+0·473	8·644	
1960	9·324	25·293	8·431	+0·733	9·897	−0·680
1961	10·004	27·573	9·191	+0·760	10·711	−0·107

Exercise 2.14

The demand for electricity in 1962 turned out to be 11·068 thousands of megawatt-hours. Use this to predict the 1963 figure by adding another line to Table 2.IV.

Exercise 2.15

The last column in Table 2.IV is obtained by subtracting the actual figure for the following year from its forecast value. Do the values of these errors (including that calculated in Exercise 2.14) suggest any change in your assumptions?

Exercise 2.16

Calculate the moving annual totals and averages for the following series of sales figures (to the nearest whole number). Also calculate the monthly trend by subtracting two successive moving averages and apply a trend correction to obtain a forecast for the following month.

Month	Sales	Sales in same month of previous year	Moving Annual Total	Moving Annual Average	Difference = Trend	Trend Correction	Fore-cast
—	—	—	2,053	171			
J	183	161					
F	187	165					
M	190	165					
A	188	168					
M	191	166					
J	190	172					
J	195	173					
A	196	176					
S	202	175					
O	203	175					
N	208	178					
D	203	179					
Annual total		2,053					

Exercise 2.17

Calculate the errors by subtracting the actual figure for each month from the forecast made in the preceding month, in Exercise 2.16.
Then answer the following:

(a) Is there any convincing evidence that the forecasts are biassed?

(b) What measure of the precision of the forecasts can you suggest?

Note on Subtracting Moving Totals

When we estimated the trend of the sales in Table 2.I as +10 per period, we appeared to use the six values from periods 5 to 10 inclusive —five in the first moving average and an extra one in the second. In fact, we used only two of the values, for periods 5 and 10, as the following analysis shows:

$$\text{Second Ma} = \tfrac{1}{5}\,(150 + 140 + 130 + 120 + 110 \qquad) = 130$$
$$\text{First MA} = \tfrac{1}{5}\,(\qquad 140 + 130 + 120 + 110 + 100) = 120$$
$$\overline{\text{Difference} = \tfrac{1}{5}\,(150 \qquad\qquad\qquad - 100) = +10}$$

The four middle values, covering periods 6 to 9, cancel out.

The method is used simply because it is convenient, and because subtracting the two extreme figures over a range of periods does something to reduce the random effects. It is inefficient because it discards a lot of the information available. You should check this point in the examples which follow.

Moving Annual Totals and Seasonal Effects

Seasonal effects usually follow an annual rhythm, because they are generated by one fundamental cause: the inclination of the earth's axis to the plane of its orbit. The effects of this occur in various ways, some being shown in Table 2.V.

TABLE 2.V

Seasonal Effects on Sales

Prime cause	Secondary cause	Examples of goods affected
Variations in sunlight	Intensity of sunlight	Sunglasses, camera films, suntan lotions
	Length of day	Lamp bulbs, premium grade petrol, theatre seats, books
Other aspects of the weather	Temperature	Coal, clothing, soft drinks, anti-freeze, contraceptives
	Rainfall	Raincoats, umbrellas, certain drugs
	Fog	Foglamps, winter cruises
Feasts, religious	Easter	Chocolate, greetings cards
	Christmas/Yule	Turkeys, fir-trees, toys, wines and spirits
pagan	Thanksgiving	Turkeys, aspirin
	Guy Fawkes' Day	Fireworks, burn dressings
political or commercial	Independence Day	Travel, resort facilities
	Bank Holidays	Tobacco
	Father's Day	

Seasonal effects are generally measured above and below the average for the year, so their total over a whole year is zero. (Sometimes the average is first adjusted for secular trend, as will be shown later.) It is for this reason that moving totals and averages are so often taken over a time-span of a single year or exact multiples of it.

Exercise 2.18

Satisfy yourself that if a manufacturer of fireworks consistently sells (in Britain) 100,000 in June, 900,000 in October and none in any other month, the Moving Annual Total of his sales is free from seasonal effects.

In Exercise 2.1 we worked out the differences between the individual sales figures in Table 1.1 and their average, on the assumption that the differences were random errors. We might also have assumed that they were seasonal effects, and there is nothing in the figures themselves to suggest which assumption is the correct one. When sales for sub-sequent years are recorded, they will often tend to confirm or deny our assumption, and it is generally true to say that at least two years' figures are needed if seasonal and random effects are to be separated.

Note on Adding Moving Averages

When a moving average is taken over an odd number of periods, the lag is always a whole number of periods—see Fig. 2.2, where

$$\text{Lag}=\tfrac{1}{2}(5-1)=2.$$

We can therefore say 'the moving average over 5 periods is a smoothed estimate of the sales in the *middle* period'.

When the number of periods is even, there is no middle period—the middle falls between two sales figures. This is awkward, and some economists get round it by adding two successive MA's to obtain a further average, like this:

Period		Sales	MA over 4 periods	Average MA
1966	J–M	78		
	A–J	62		
	J–S←	57	67	67·5
	O–D	71	68	
1967	J–M	82		

Each MA has been written opposite the middle of the time span over which it was taken. The average MA corresponds conveniently to the third quarter of 1966.

Now let us analyse it:

$$67\cdot5=\tfrac{1}{2}(67+68)=\tfrac{1}{2}\times 67+\tfrac{1}{2}\times 68$$
$$67=\tfrac{1}{4}(78+62+57+71)$$
$$68=\tfrac{1}{4}(62+57+71+82)$$
$$\tfrac{1}{2}\times 67=\tfrac{1}{8}\times 78+\tfrac{1}{8}\times 62+\tfrac{1}{8}\times 57+\tfrac{1}{8}\times 71$$

D

$$\tfrac{1}{2} \times 68 = \tfrac{1}{8} \times 62 + \tfrac{1}{8} \times 57 + \tfrac{1}{8} \times 71 + \tfrac{1}{8} \times 82$$

$$\text{So } 67{\cdot}5 = \tfrac{1}{8} \times 78 + \tfrac{1}{4} \times 62 + \tfrac{1}{4} \times 57 + \tfrac{1}{4} \times 71 + \tfrac{1}{8} \times 82$$

$$= \tfrac{1}{4}(\tfrac{1}{2} \times 78 + 62 + 57 + 71 + \tfrac{1}{2} \times 82)$$

The average MA is therefore equivalent to an MA taken over *five* periods, but after the first and last sales figures have been halved. Such a procedure can be justified sometimes, as in averaging stock levels where it corresponds to Simpson's rule for estimating areas. It is of doubtful validity when applied to sales figures.

Any man who sets out to average averages should clearly recognize the implications of what he is doing by analysing a typical case, as above.

Estimating Secular and Seasonal Trends

The quarterly sales of wool to a manufacturer of knitwear in 1966 were:

TABLE 2.VI

		Sales	Deviations from average
1966	Jan.–Mar.	78	+11
	Apr.–Jun.	62	−5
	Jul.–Sep.	57	−10
	Oct.–Dec.	71	+4
	Total	268	0
	Average	67	

We can assume, if we choose, that there are no trends at all. Then all the deviations are random; the best forecast for the first quarter of 1966 is 67; the standard deviation is 9·3; the confidence limits are ±19, so the forecast is likely to lie between 48 and 86. When the figure for the next quarter turns out to be 82, the assumptions seem to be reasonable.

Nevertheless, the low precision of the forecast may lead us to look for an improvement. Suppose we assume that there is no secular trend but that seasonal effects may occur. There are two possible justifications for this assumption: first, sales of woollen goods are affected by weather; secondly, the observed deviations follow the sequence + − − + rather than + − + − or − + − +. The deviations are then taken as estimates of the seasonal effects, the first quarter being 11 higher than the average and so on. With no secular trend, our best forecast is that the first quarter of 1967 will be 78, the same as for the first quarter of 1966.

We may wish to make the reasonable assumption that both seasonal and random effects occur; unfortunately, the limited information at our disposal does not help us to unscramble them without making still more assumptions which would largely be guesswork.

When more information comes in, in the form of the first quarterly sales return for 1967, we can utilize it in at least two ways. We might halve the error between the forecast (78) and the actual (82) and reason as follows. The base level of sales is 67. The 'true' seasonal effect in Jan.–Mar. 1966 was $+13$; the random error was -2. The best forecast for Jan.–Mar. 1967 was $67 + 13 = 80$. The actual sales included a random error of $+2$. In doing this, we are following a general principle that random errors will usually add up to zero.

Instead of doing this, we shall use the extra information to estimate the secular trend from the difference of two successive moving averages. Substituting 82 for 78 gives a new MA of 68, an increase of $+1$. The secular trend is therefore $+1$ for each period. How will this affect our estimates of the seasonal effects?

Look at the following set of figures:

TABLE 2.VII

		Seasonally-corrected MAA
1966	Jan.–Mar.	65·5
	Apr.–Jun.	66·5
	Jul.–Sep.	67·5
	Oct.–Dec.	68·5
	Total	268·0
	Average	67·0

They show the correct increase of $+1$ from one period to the next and their average agrees with that already found for 1966. Figure 2.5 shows how they were calculated: the middle of the first quarter occurs $1\frac{1}{2}$ periods before the middle of the year, so if we want to include the effects of secular trend we must subtract $1\frac{1}{2} \times (+1)$, giving 65·5 as shown above.

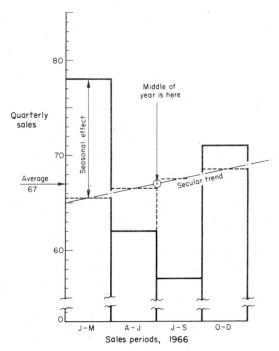

Figure 2.5 Effect of secular trends on estimates of seasonal effects

We now have an estimate of what the sales would have been in the first quarter if there had been no seasonal effect. For this reason we call 65·5 a **seasonally-corrected** figure. The seasonal effect is then obtained from the difference $78 - 65·5 = 12·5$. (Now estimate the seasonal effects for the other three periods, using Figure 2.5.)

Projecting the seasonally-corrected figures forward along the line labelled 'secular trend', we find that the first quarter of 1967 gives 69·5; the seasonal effect is $+12·5$, giving 82 as the actual sales and thus checking the arithmetic.

We are now in a position to forecast the remaining three periods for 1967 and the first in 1968.

The actual sales are given for comparison, and we see from the last two quarters that our estimate of the secular trend may have been rather low. This is not surprising since it was based on such scanty information.

TABLE 2.VIII

Period	Seasonally corrected estimate	Seasonal effect	Forecast sales	Actual sales
1967 Apr.–Jun.	70·5	– 4·5	66	64
Jul.–Sep.	71·5	– 10·5	61	61
Oct.–Dec.	72·5	+ 2·5	75	81
1968 Jan.–Mar.	73·5	+ 12·5	86	92
		Total	288	298

As each new quarterly figure comes in, we can if we wish revise the estimates of secular trend and seasonal effects and, as we accumulate more and more figures, begin to record errors, calculate standard deviations and set up confidence limits.

One can devise continuous sales forecasting systems of this type, but they are not very common; the amounts of data and calculation are rather great for human operation. This objection may be overcome by using an electronic computer, but a counter-argument then arises: the trend-estimating methods described here are crude. If a computer is to be used, one of the more advanced techniques such as regression analysis would be more appropriate.

Note on the Lag in Obtaining Data

Some practical readers will by now be feeling unhappy about one of my own tacit assumptions, which is that figures can be collected, calculated and applied instantaneously—that we can use the data for the first quarter of 1966 to forecast sales in the second quarter.

The assumption has simplified some of the explanation, and in fact does not cause any serious difficulties. I have tended to concentrate on the forecast for one period ahead, but all the procedures are valid for more than one period. Table 2.VII can be extended indefinitely by adding the current estimate of trend, + 1, for each extra period. Table 2.VIII shows forecasts for three periods ahead, so if the first quarter's figures for 1967 were not available until the end of April, we could still go ahead and forecast the sales for July to September.

So a time-lag of one period in obtaining sales figures and revising the current forecast is simply equivalent to forecasting the next period but one.

Other Aspects of Moving Averages

The techniques of using moving averages for forecasting has developed beyond what is described here. They can be used to generate a smoothed estimate of a trend, to find the 'trend of a trend' and to incorporate multiplicative as well as additive effects. The value of these extensions is open to doubt; all their refinements cannot compensate for the underlying crudeness of the initial estimates of trend. Elaborate computation based on moving averages is like carving unseasoned wood.

There is, however, one development of the technique which deserves close attention, and that is **weighting**—in particular, **exponential weighting**. Its practical applications are many and they are spreading; it can be used to simplify calculation and reduce data storage; it therefore deserves a chapter to itself, which follows.

3 WEIGHTED MOVING AVERAGES

Weighting in General

When we take an average, we add up all the values we wish to include and divide by the number of values used. (If we were to divide by any other number, we should bias the average upwards or downwards.)

Take for example the sales in Table 3.I, already used in Chapter 2 (page 37). We shall consider the MAA taken over periods 2 to 5 inclusive, which is 68.

$$\text{Then } 68 = \tfrac{1}{4}(62 + 57 + 71 + 82)$$

By clearing the bracket, we can write

$$68 = \tfrac{1}{4} \times 62 + \tfrac{1}{4} \times 57 + \tfrac{1}{4} \times 71 + \tfrac{1}{4} \times 82$$

and we may describe the process of averaging in the following way:

'Multiply every sales figure which contributes to the average by a factor and add the answers to obtain the average.'

The factors in the example just given all add up to one, and a little thought will show that this condition *must* be observed if the average is not to be biassed. They are also equal: we can interpret this by saying that all four sales figures are given the same importance or weight. The factors are therefore called **weights** and the process of determining their size is called **weighting**.

TABLE 3.I

Period		No.	Sales	MAA
1966	J–M	1	78	
	A–J	2	62	
	J–S	3	57	
	O–D	4	71	67
1967	J–M	5	82	68

Exercise 3.1

In calculating the MA above, 68, what weights were given to the sales in periods 1 and 2?

Rectangular Weighting

The moving totals considered so far have all had equal or, more strictly, **rectangular weighting**; this is illustrated in Figure 3.1 (*a*), where the height of each column represents *not* the sales figure, but its

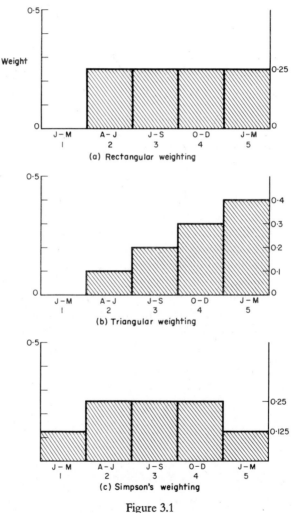

(a) Rectangular weighting

(b) Triangular weighting

(c) Simpson's weighting

Figure 3.1
Types of weighting

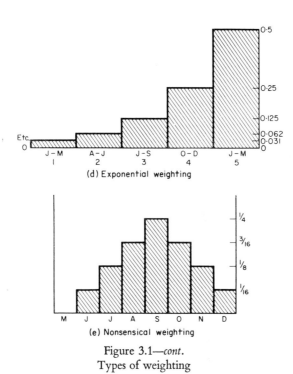

(d) Exponential weighting

(e) Nonsensical weighting

Figure 3.1—*cont.*
Types of weighting

weight (or importance). Rectangular weighting has the merit of
simplicity, and it accords with the conventional method of taking an
average. In certain cases it is also free, as we have seen, from bias
introduced by seasonal effects. Even so, it has some unsatisfactory
features. The figure for period 2 is nearly a year old, and yet it ranks as
equal in importance to the most modern one, that for period 5.
Again, period 2 is considered to have some importance, although it is
nearly a year old—yet no weight at all is given to period 1, just over a
year ago. This is a rather sudden loss of weight as the moving average
advances.

Triangular Weighting

Triangular weighting gives a greater weight to the most recent
sales figure, as shown in Fig. 3.1 (*b*). The weights shown are 0, 0·1,

0·2, 0·3, 0·4. Applied to the first four periods in Table 3.I, they give:

$$0·1 \times 78 = 7·8$$
$$0·2 \times 62 = 12·4$$
$$0·3 \times 57 = 17·1$$
$$0·4 \times 71 = 28·4$$

Weighted Moving Average $= \overline{65·7}$

The method is not so convenient as rectangular weighting, because one cannot easily revise a previous average.

Exercise 3.2

(*a*) Calculate the triangularly-weighted moving average for periods 2 to 5 inclusive in Table 3.I.

(*b*) Does it differ from the rectangularly-weighted moving average, and if so, what explanation can you offer?

The result of Exercise 3.2 (*b*) tells us that seasonal variations will usually impart a seasonal bias to the triangularly-weighted moving average.

For those who would like to try this method on their own data, sets of weights are given in Table 3.II.

TABLE 3.II

Sets of Triangular Weights

Period	Number of periods to be covered									
	3	4	5	6	7	8	9	10	12	13
1st	17	10	7	5	4	3	2	2	1	1
2nd	33	20	13	9	7	6	4	4	3	2
3rd	50	30	20	14	11	8	7	5	4	3
4th		40	27	19	14	11	9	7	5	4
5th			33	24	18	14	11	9	6	6
6th				29	21	17	13	11	8	7
7th					25	19	16	13	9	8
8th						22	18	15	10	9
9th							20	16	12	10
10th								18	13	11
11th									14	12
12th									15	13
13th										14

Note: The totals obtained by the use of these weights should be divided by 100.

Exercise 3.3

Select any column in Table 3.II and find the total of the weights in it.

Simpson's Weighting

Simpson's weighting, shown in Figure 3.1 (*c*), is applied automatically when two successive moving averages are themselves averaged (as discussed in Chapter 2). It has the advantage that it will not impart a seasonal bias to the average if the periods are suitably chosen: the diagram shows that the *total* weight given to the first quarter of the year is the same as that given to the other three. All four quarters being equally represented, any seasonal variations will cancel each other out.

The indiscriminate averaging of averages will often yield nonsensical weightings such as in Figure 3.1 (*e*). This is taken from an actual case: a company calculated moving averages over four periods and then, in pursuit of even greater smoothing, averaged four successive averages. The final effect was as shown, and it cannot be justified by any rational argument. Note, though, that the weights still add up to one.

Exponential Weighting

Figure 3.1 (*d*) shows a set of weights which resemble triangular ones in that recent sales are given more importance than older ones. Unlike triangular weights, they differ by a constant *ratio*, called the **common ratio** instead of a constant *quantity*: the weight for period 4 is half that for period 5, and so on. In consequence, the final average includes, in theory, all past sales figures; in practice, some of the weights are negligibly small. The weights in Figure 3.1 (*d*) outline an exponential curve, and the system is therefore called **exponential weighting.** (The term **geometrical weighting** is sometimes used because the weights form a geometrical progression. The weight for any period is always the same fraction of that for the next period and this fraction is called the common ratio.) The method by which it is applied is often referred to as **Holt's method.**

Exercise 3.4

In Figure 3.1 (*d*) what would be the weights for the two periods preceding period 1? The answers should be given to two decimal places.

At first sight, we might reject exponential weighting on the grounds that it is too cumbersome to calculate. Paradoxically, it turns out to be even easier than an ordinary MA.

Suppose we have an existing exponentially weighted moving average (EWMA) calculated as in Table 3.III.

TABLE 3.III

(Note that the most recent period is given first)

Period		Weight	Sales	Weight × Sales
1967	J–M	0·500	82	41·0
1966	O–D	0·250	71	17·8
	J–S	0·125	57	7·1
	A–J	0·062	62	3·8
	J–M	0·031	78	2·4
1965	O–D	0·016	69	1·1
	J–S	0·008	58	0·5
	A–J	0·004	59	0·2
	J–M	0·002	75	0·2
1964	O–D	0·001	73	0·1
		0·999	EWMA	74·2

Later, the figure for 1967 April to June comes in: it is 64. This is now the figure for the most recent period, so its weight is 0·5 and we could go on to compile Table 3.IV.

TABLE 3.IV

Period		Weight	Sales	Weight × Sales
1967	A–J	0·500	64	32·0
	J–M	0·250	82	20·5
1966	O–D	0·125	71	8·9
	J–S	0·062	57	3·6
	A–J	0·031	62	1·9
	J–M	0·016	78	1·2
1965	O–D	0·008	69	0·6
	J–S	0·004	58	0·2
	A–J	0·002	59	0·1
	J–M	0·001	75	0·1
			New EWMA	69·1

But this is all unnecessary! All the sales figures from Table 3.III have been brought forward (except the last, 73, because its weight is now negligible) but each now has just half the weight it had before.

We could achieve the same result by simply bringing forward half their total. The calculation would then become

$$\text{New EWMA} = 0.5 \times \text{New Sales Figure}$$
$$+ 0.5 \times \text{Old EWMA}$$
$$= 0.5 \times 64 + 0.5 \times 74.2$$
$$= 32.0 + 37.1 = 69.1$$

Exercise 3.5

The sales figure for 1967 July to September turns out to be 61. Calculate the new EWMA.

Note on Labelling Periods

So far, we have labelled periods sequentially, with period 2 following period 1 and so on. This is a logical way, but it can be inconvenient. We often want to look backwards in time, and especially when considering exponential weighting. Negative numbers make this easier, so we shall label the period in the immediate past as '– 1', the one before that as '– 2' and so on. The current period then becomes 'period 0', the next in the immediate future is 'period 1' and so on.

Generalizing the Rule

We started with a common ratio of 0.5 because it is easy to explain. It also has the merit, for demonstration, of exaggerating the 'dying-away' effect of exponential weighting: one has only to go about ten periods into the past to find all previous sales figures contributing virtually nothing to the average. Such rapid decay of importance is not always desirable, and other exponential weightings will now be considered.

Exercise 3.6

Consider the following weights:

Period		
– 1	0.200
– 2	0.160
– 3	0.128

$$\text{Period } \begin{array}{cc} -4 & 0\cdot102 \\ -5 & 0\cdot082 \\ -6 & 0\cdot066 \\ -7 & 0\cdot052 \end{array}$$

(a) Have they a common ratio? If so, what is it?

(b) What would be the weights for the periods -8, -9 and -10?

(c) What is the total of the weights for the ten periods?

(d) Draw a bar chart of the weights, similar to Figure 3.1 (d) but covering 10 periods, and sketch in Figure 3.1 (d) on the same scale for comparison.

The rule for producing a new EWMA from an old one may be generalized into

New EWMA = $a \times$ New Sales Figure + $b \times$ Old EWMA.

It can be proved that if all the individual weights are to add up to 1, then a and b must also add up to 1. In other words, $b = 1 - a$. (In technical literature, the Greek alpha, a, is almost universally used instead of a.) The factor b is equal to the common ratio.

Exercise 3.7

Suppose you want to construct a set of exponential weights in which the weight assigned to each period was 10 per cent greater than that for the preceding period. What value would you give to a (the weight of the most recent sales figure)?

Choosing the Weighting Factors

EWMA's, like MA's, are only a satisfactory method of smoothing when the secular and seasonal trends are small in comparison with the random fluctuations. If the figures show a systematic trend, their EWMA will lag.

Exercise 3.8

Calculate EWMA's for the sales in Table 2.I, starting with an old EWMA of 100 and putting $a = \frac{1}{3}$. Plot the results as a graph similar to Figure 2.1.

Exercise 3.9

The following table continues the series given in Table 3.IV.

Period		Period No. (0)	Sales
1966	J–M	1	78
	A–J	2	62
	J–S	3	57
	O–D	4	71
1967	J–M	5	82
	A–J	6	64
	J–S	7	61
	O–D	8	81
1968	J–M	9	92
	A–J	10	69
	J–S	11	63
	O–D	12	85

Taking a as 0·4 and starting with an EWMA of 75 in period 0, calculate EWMAs for these figures. Draw a graph showing
(*a*) the sales themselves, (*b*) their rectangular MAs, (*c*) their EWMAs.

The time-lag is greater when the common ratio b is high, but a high ratio is also associated with better smoothing. So we have the same conflict of smoothing versus lag as occurs in rectangular MAs.

A simple formula relates the two. An EWMA will achieve the same amount of smoothing as a rectangular MA taken over N periods if

$$b = \frac{N-1}{N+1}$$

It then follows that

$$a = \frac{2}{N+1}$$

and

$$N = \frac{2}{a} - 1.$$

Exercise 3.10

You are already using a moving annual average of (calendar) monthly sales but you propose to replace it by an EWMA. What value of a would give you the same amount of smoothing? What would be the corresponding common ratio?

For an established product as distinct from a new one, a, in practice, is often given a value of 0.1, 0.15 or 0.2. In other words, the smoothing effect is about the same as that obtained from a monthly MAA. Probably the commonest value is 0.1, which makes for ease of computation. It is equivalent to a rectangularly-weighted MA taken over 19 periods, so it tends to be more heavily **damped** than a monthly MAA.

Damping is a measure of the extent to which a MAA responds to changes in the new values incorporated in it. A **heavy damping** implies a long time-lag in response to a change, and is obtained by selecting a low value for a.

Higher values are sometimes given to a, especially when past data are inadequate. One virtue of the EWMA is that one can start with a guess and gradually reduce the extent to which it affects the average by incorporating real sales data as they are received.

Exercise 3.11

You are introducing a new product and have no previous sales figures to work on; market research has given a provisional figure of 50 items a month. The actual sales are as in the table below. Calculate an exponentially weighted moving average for each month, giving a weight of $\frac{1}{3}$ to the new actual sales and a weight of $\frac{2}{3}$ to the old forecast. List the errors.

Month	Sales	Forecast (EWMA)		Error (Forecast – Actual)
		50	(J)	
J	101		(F)	– 51
F	103		(M)	
M	101		(A)	
A	102		(M)	
M	98		(J)	
J	102		(J)	
J	101		(A)	
A	102		(S)	
S	99		(O)	
O	97		(N)	
N	98		(D)	
D	97		(J)	

Exponential Weighting and Secular Trends

The difference between two successive EWMA's is an estimate of the secular trend, as it was for rectangular MA's. See, for example,

Figure S3.2 in the solution to Exercise 3.8: if the sales trend (marked 'actual' in the figure) had continued upwards after period 15, the EWMA curve would have continued to follow it with a lag of two periods but along a line which ultimately becomes parallel to it. In other words, the rate of growth of the EWMA—the secular trend, in fact—would be the same as for the actual sales.

Exercise 3.12

Test the above statement by altering the sales figures in the solution to Exercise 3.8. For period 16 put 210 instead of 200, for period 17 put 220 and so on. Compare the difference between successive EWMA's with the difference between successive months' sales. (Work to one decimal place.)

The trend estimated in this way may be used to calculate a trend correction for forecasting by the same methods as for rectangular MA's. We can smooth out fluctuations by averaging successive estimates of the trend, and use exponential weightings in so doing: these methods have been described in detail by Brown [1] and by Coutie and his co-authors. [9]

Exponential Weighting and Seasonal Trends

If the individual sales periods are fractions of a year, seasonal effects will be reflected in them: they will be damped down but the effect may still be considerable. Suppose, for instance, that we are looking at sales of greetings cards, for which the seasonal peak occurs in December. At the end of the year, the December sales will contribute more to an EWMA than will any other month, so any forecast derived from the EWMA will be biassed upwards. Six months later, the June sales will have more weight than those for December; the bias will now be downwards.

These effects were seen in the solution to Exercise 3.9, and Figure S3.3 shows them graphically: it also shows how the rectangular MA remains unaffected by seasonal fluctuation.

There are methods for correcting this—Winters's [5] for example—but once again we can say that if we wish to make complex forecasts incorporating secular and seasonal trends (and possibly others), rigorous statistical methods will give a better answer. They are described in the following chapters.

E

4 REGRESSION ANALYSIS

Fitting Straight Lines

When we estimated the trend by subtracting two successive moving averages, we used only two figures out of a whole series, and ignored the others (see page 35). Look at the figures in Table 4.I: since they are for an obsolescent type of gramophone record, they may reasonably be assumed to have a trend—a downward one. These values are shown as a graph in Figure 4.1, the broken line being the mean.

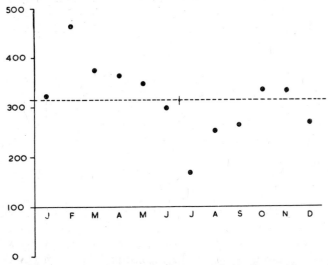

Figure 4.1 Production of 78 rpm records (in thousands)

We could estimate the trend by subtracting the last figure from the first and dividing by the number of intervals between them: 11, not 12. The estimate would be $\frac{1}{11}$ (270 – 324) i.e. – 4·91, the negative sign showing that the trend is downwards. We could also use other pairs of figures, e.g. those for period 11 and 2:

$$\frac{336 - 463}{9} = - 14·11$$

They give a very different estimate, and it would be useful if we could combine all twelve figures in some way so as to obtain a 'best'

TABLE 4.I

Production of 78 rpm Gramophone Records in Great Britain, 1960

Month	Period	Production (in thousands)
January	1	324
February	2	463
March	3	374
April	4	363
May	5	349
June	6	302
July	7	169
August	8	256
September	9	263
October	10	334
November	11	336
December	12	270
	Total	3,803
	Average	316·9

estimate of the trend. To do so, we use a **least squares method**, and define our problem as follows.

How can we fit a straight line through the points in Figure 4·1 so that the sum of the squares of the deviations is made as small as possible? Fig. 4·2 shows this problem graphically, the arrowed lines being some of the deviations. The method of solving the problem was

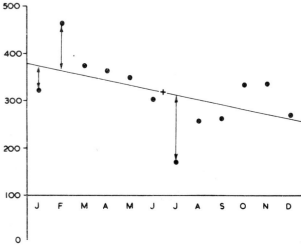

Figure 4.2 Production of 78 rpm records with linear trend line

devised by the nineteenth-century statistician Galton, who applied it
to the relationship between the heights of fathers and their sons. He
showed that although tall fathers tend to have tall sons, there is a
regression to the mean. In this way the rather inappropriate name
regression analysis was derived.

Fitting a Trend Line by Eye

Before going on to consider the arithmetic of regression analysis,
let us look at what happens when a line is fitted by eye. We move a
ruler or thread over the graph with a mixture of lateral and rotational
adjustments until it 'looks about right'.

Sometimes we also apply common-sense rules: for example, that there
should be about as many dots below the line as above (check whether
this is so in Fig. 4·2). One helpful rule, which is not widely known, is
that the best-fitting line passes through the point which corresponds to
the two averages. In Table 4.I, the 'average period' is $6\frac{1}{2}$, halfway
between June and July and the average sales are 316·9. The cross in
Figure 4.2 is the corresponding point; having marked it, we have only
to stick a pin into it and rotate the ruler about it. This method reduces
fitting by eye to one sort of movement of the ruler instead of two, but
it is still crude compared with regression analysis.

Calculating the Slope

Since it can be proved mathematically that the best-fitting straight
line passes through the point corresponding to the two means, we only
need to find its slope or trend to define the line unambiguously. The
slope is known as its **linear regression coefficient**, and one method
of calculating it is shown in Table 4.II.

The weight assigned to each period is its deviation from the 'average
period' (6·5 in this case) and is given in column (3). Sets of weights for
any number of periods up to 12 are given in Table 4.III on p. 58.

The values we are working on are given in column (5), and column
(4) shows how each is made up from a 'base value' and a trend, as was
explained in Chapter 2.

The value for each period is multiplied by the weight for that
period: the results are given in column (6) and their total, − 1,464·5, is
the numerator.

If each weight in column (3) is squared and the squares are added up, we get the denominator, in this case 143 (see also Table 4.III). The linear regression coefficient is then found by dividing the numerator by the denominator: it is − 10·24.

TABLE 4.II

Production of 78 rpm Records: Calculation of Linear Regression Coefficient

Month	No.	Weight	Production (in thousands) Components	Value	Value × Weight	Interpolated Value	Error
(1)	(2)	(3)	(4)	(5)	(6)	(7)	(8)
J	1	− 5·5	$p − 5·5t$	324	− 1,782	373	− 49
F	2	− 4·5	$p − 4·5t$	463	− 2,083·5	363	+ 100
M	3	− 3·5	$p − 3·5t$	374	− 1,309	353	+ 21
A	4	− 2·5	$p − 2·5t$	363	− 907·5	342	+ 21
M	5	− 1·5	$p − 1·5t$	349	− 523·5	332	+ 17
J	6	− 0·5	$p − 0·5t$	302	− 151	322	− 20
J	7	+ 0·5	$p + 0·5t$	169	+ 84·5	312	− 143
A	8	+ 1·5	$p + 1·5t$	256	+ 384	302	− 46
S	9	+ 2·5	$p + 2·5t$	263	+ 657·5	291	− 28
O	10	+ 3·5	$p + 3·5t$	334	+ 1,169	281	+ 53
N	11	+ 4·5	$p + 4·5t$	336	+ 1,512	271	+ 65
D	12	+ 5·5	$p + 5·5t$	270	+ 1,485	261	+ 9

Total   78   0 $12p$ 3,808   **− 1,464·5 = Numerator**
Average   6·5 p 316·9
Sum of squares of weights = **143 = Denominator**

Linear Regression Coefficient $= \dfrac{− 1,464·5}{143} = − 10·24 = t$

The negative sign means that the trend is downwards: in other words, the production of 78 rpm records is declining at an average rate of 10,240 per month.

Column (7) in Table 4.II shows the values which lie along the trend line, or 'regression line' as it is called. Each value is calculated by assembling the components given in column (4), where t stands for the trend. Thus, for March we have

Average $= p = 316·9$
$− 3·5t = − 3·5 × − 10·24 = + 35·8$
Interpolated Value $= 316·9 + 35·8 = 352·7$
rounded to 353

The actual value was 374, which is 21 greater. Assuming no seasonal effects, we may call this a random error: the complete set of such errors is given in column (8). From it we may, if we wish, calculate the variance, standard deviation and confidence limits associated with any forecast.

One important difference between this method and those which preceded it is that we know something about the random errors before we even begin to forecast. There is no need to wait for comparisons between forecast and actual values in order to assess the reliability of our methods.

TABLE 4.III

Weights and Sums of Squares for Linear Regression

Number of Periods:	3	4	5	6	7	8	9	10	11	12	13
	-1	$-1{\cdot}5$	-2	$-2{\cdot}5$	-3	$-3{\cdot}5$	-4	$-4{\cdot}5$	-5	$-5{\cdot}5$	-6
	0	$-0{\cdot}5$	-1	$-1{\cdot}5$	-2	$-2{\cdot}5$	-3	$-3{\cdot}5$	-4	$-4{\cdot}5$	-5
	$+1$	$+0{\cdot}5$	0	$-0{\cdot}5$	-1	$-1{\cdot}5$	-2	$-2{\cdot}5$	-3	$-3{\cdot}5$	-4
		$+1{\cdot}5$	$+1$	$+0{\cdot}5$	0	$-0{\cdot}5$	-1	$-1{\cdot}5$	-2	$-2{\cdot}5$	-3
			$+2$	$+1{\cdot}5$	$+1$	$+0{\cdot}5$	0	$-0{\cdot}5$	-1	$-1{\cdot}5$	-2
				$+2{\cdot}5$	$+2$	$+1{\cdot}5$	$+1$	$+0{\cdot}5$	0	$-0{\cdot}5$	-1
Weights					$+3$	$+2{\cdot}5$	$+2$	$+1{\cdot}5$	$+1$	$+0{\cdot}5$	0
						$+3{\cdot}5$	$+3$	$+2{\cdot}5$	$+2$	$+1{\cdot}5$	$+1$
							$+4$	$+3{\cdot}5$	$+3$	$+2{\cdot}5$	$+2$
								$+4{\cdot}5$	$+4$	$+3{\cdot}5$	$+3$
									$+5$	$+4{\cdot}5$	$+4$
										$+5{\cdot}5$	$+5$
											$+6$
Denominator = Sum of Squares of *Weights*	2	5	10	17·5	28	42	60	82·5	110	143	182

Forecasting by Regression

We referred to the number obtained by adding the appropriate multiple of the trend to the base value as the **interpolated value**, because it lies within the time span over which the regression coefficient (trend) was calculated. Going outside this time span is called **extrapolation**. There is usually no point in extrapolating backwards, but to extrapolate into the future is, in fact, forecasting.

Nothing could be more simple. The series of figures in column (7) of Table 4.II has a common difference of − 10·24 (which rounds off to − 10 and occasionally − 11). We can continue the series indefinitely, using the following procedure:

1. Take the number of the period for which the forecast is required, e.g. January 1961 is 13, February is 14.
2. Subtract 6·5 (the 'average period').
3. Multiply the answer by the *t*-value (− 10·24).
4. Add the product to the average (316·9). In this case we have a negative product and must *subtract*.
5. Round off.

This gives, for January 1961,

$$316·9 - 6·5 \times 10·24 = 250·3, \text{ say } 250$$

and for February

$$316·9 - 7·5 \times 10·24 = 240·1, \text{ say } 240$$

and for March

$$316·9 - 8·5 \times 10·24 = 229·9, \text{ say } 230.$$

Exercise 4.1

Assuming that the figure in Table 2.IV have a linear trend, calculate the trend over the period 1956–1961 inclusive, using the method shown in Table 4.II (but omitting the calculation of residual errors).

Exercise 4.2

Use the results of the previous exercise to forecast the production of electricity in 1962 and 1963.

Extrapolation to Zero

From our analysis of the production of gramophone records, we could deduce the time at which production will become zero.

A production of 316·9 in the middle of 1960, declining at 10·24 a month, would reach zero in 316·9 ÷ 10·24, which is 31 months, or February 1963. This is obviously the limit to which we can stretch the linear trend, since to go beyond it would imply negative production.

Such absurdities often occur: a straight line may be a reasonable approximation but only for a restricted period. It would be better, if we wanted to project the production of gramophone records more than a few periods into the future, to assume a ratio (that is, exponential) trend.

TABLE 4.IV

Logarithms of Production of Gramophone Records

Month	Period	Production	Logarithm
January	1	324	2·5105
February	2	463	2·6656
March	3	374	2·5729
April	4	363	2·5599
May	5	349	2·5428
June	6	302	2·4800
July	7	169	2·2279
August	8	256	2·4082
September	9	263	2·4200
October	10	334	2·5237
November	11	336	2·5263
December	12	270	2·4314

		Total	29·8693
		Mean	2·4891
		Antilogarithm of Mean	308·4

We have already seen (in Table 1.II) the effect of changing an assumption in this way. It generally makes little difference when the trend is not very steep and figures are interpolated: the ratio trend curve in Figure 4.3 is barely distinguishable from the additive trend curve in Figure 4.2. The difference between the two becomes greater, however, when they are extrapolated.

Exercise 4.3

When will the trend curve in Figure 4.3 reach zero?

Logarithmic Transformation

The ratio trend curve in Figure 4.3 can be fitted by using linear regression on the *logarithms* of the sales instead of on the sales themselves. Suppose that sales are increasing by 6·5 per cent every year: then the sales in any year will be 1·065 times those in the previous year (see Exercise A.21, page 117). Then since

Next year's sales $= 1 \cdot 065 \times$ This year's sales,

it follows that, since log $1 \cdot 065 = 0 \cdot 0273$

log (Next year's sales) $= 0 \cdot 0273 +$ log (This year's sales)

or, in logarithmic terms, there is a constant additive trend.

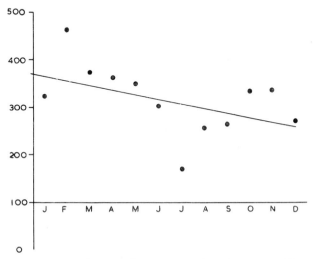

Figure 4.3 Production of 78 rpm records with ratio trend line

In order to understand this manipulation and the working which follows it, you may need to brush up your knowledge of logarithms. An Appendix is provided for this purpose on page 103.

Exercise 4.4

If sales were *decreasing* by 6·5 per cent a year, what would be the trend of the log sales?

Turning a figure into its logarithm is often called a **logarithmic transformation**. Table 4.IV shows the logarithmic transformation of the figures in Table 4.I. Their 'mean' is 308·4, which is lower than the arithmetic mean (316·9): it is the **geometric mean**, which would be obtained by multiplying together all the figures in Table 4.I and taking their twelfth root.

If the logarithms in Table 4.IV are put into column (5) of Table 4.II and exactly the same calculation carried out, we get

Sum of new figures (log × weight) in column (6)
$$= -1.9115$$

$$\text{Linear Regression Coefficient} = -\frac{1.9115}{143} = -0.01337$$

(Subtracting 0·01337 from 0 to obtain a positive mantissa—see p. 107)

$$0 - 0.01337 = \bar{1}.98663$$
$$\text{Antilog } \bar{1}.98663 = 0.9697$$

So, the figure for any month is 0·9697 that of the previous month and the percentage reduction every month will be 100 (1 − 0·9697) = 3·03 per cent.

We can now interpolate the regression values just as we did for column (7) of Table 4.II and compute the differences shown in the last column. From these differences, it is possible to calculate the standard deviation, which is 0·103, and hence the 95 per cent confidence limits, ±0·206. Now the antilog of +0·206 is 1·61 and of −0·206 ($\bar{1}$·794) is 0·62; in other words, the upper limit is 61 per cent higher than the forecast itself and the lower is 38 per cent below it. (It should be reiterated here that these calculations are only approximate.)

Forecasting by extrapolation is now a simple matter: it is done as for the additive trend on page 59. For example, suppose we wish to forecast the first quarter of 1961:

	Forecast=
	Antilog
January: 2·4891 + (6·5 × − 0·01337) = 2·4023	252
February: January Figure − 0·01337 = 2·3889	245
March: February Figure − 0·01337 = 2·3756	237

Exercise 4.5

Compare the forecasts made by extrapolation of the additive trend (page 59) with those from the ratio trend.

It is in the longer term that the difference between the two trends becomes most evident. In February 1963, when we found that production would be zero with an additive trend, a ratio trend would forecast 116.

Forecasting Halving or Doubling of Present Sales

A knowledge of the ratio trend makes it easy for us to forecast the time at which present sales will halve or double themselves.

Taking 'present' to mean 'at the middle of 1960', we have, for 78 rpm records,

$$(0 \cdot 9697)^n = 0 \cdot 5$$

where n is the number of periods by which production will halve.

$$n \log 0 \cdot 9697 = \log 0 \cdot 5$$
$$n = \frac{\log 0 \cdot 5}{\log 0 \cdot 9697} = \frac{\bar{1} \cdot 6990}{\bar{1} \cdot 9866} = \frac{-0 \cdot 3010}{-0 \cdot 01337}$$
$$= 22 \cdot 5$$

The answer would be 'in May 1962'. Half the geometric mean for 1960 is 154: the actual figure for May 1962 was 165, and the average for April, May and June 1962 was 158.

If sales are increasing, a similar method, using log 2 instead of log 0·5, will give the number of periods in which sales will double.

Exercise 4.6

Assuming a ratio trend, use the data in Table 2.IV to forecast the demand for electricity in 1962 and 1963.

Exercise 4.7

It has been said that the demand for electricity in Great Britain doubles itself every ten years. Use the ratio trend to check this statement.

Exercise 4.8

What is the percentage increase in demand per year?

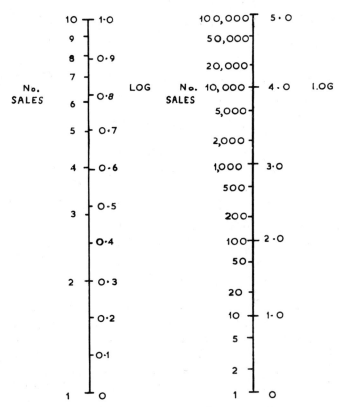

Figure 4.4 Logarithmic transformation scales

Transformation Scales

   Logarithms may be taken from tables in the usual way, but may also be read off from transformation scales as shown in Figure 4.4. The logarithm of 2, for instance, is 0·3010, so whatever the distance from 1 to 10 may be, the calibration for number 2 is marked at 0·3010 of this distance from the origin. Number 1 is calibrated at the origin itself, because its logarithm is zero. By using a logarithmic scale of numbers vertically, we can in effect plot the logarithms directly from the numbers. The horizontal time scale will be drawn with ordinary linear intervals. Graph-paper calibrated in this way is known as **semi-log paper**, and is often used for plotting figures with a ratio trend, because the trend line becomes straight after this transformation: this is illustrated in Figure 4.5. Semi-log paper ('semi' because only the vertical scale is logarithmic) may have one or more **cycles** on the vertical scale. The example shown in Figure 4.5 has one cycle, from

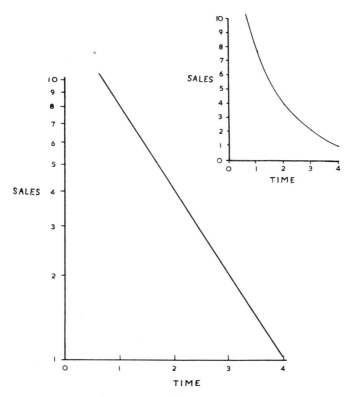

Figure 4.5 Ratio trend line on semi-log paper and (inset) on ordinary squared paper

1 to 10: it would be useful for plotting the gramophone record data, with the vertical scale calibrated from 100 to 1,000. The electricity data in Table 2.IV (page 34) calls for two-cycle paper calibrated as 1–10–100 as in Figure 4.6. Some data may need three- or even four-cycle paper to make plotting convenient.

Semi-log paper may be used for fitting and extrapolating curves by

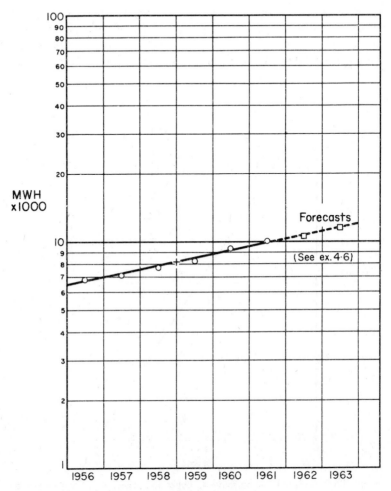

Figure 4.6 Production of electricity, on two-cycle semi-log paper

eye, but it has its pitfalls. For one thing, the best curve passes through the *geometric* mean of the sales but the *arithmetic* mean of the time; for another, small variations in its slope can generate big errors when extrapolated. It is best used for *summarizing* analyses of sales in pictorial form rather than for performing the analysis. In particular, it is useful for comparing rates of growth in items which may sell in greatly differing quantities; if the semi-log graphs are parallel, the two items have the same ratio trend, i.e. rate of growth. Such a situation could occur when a new item is being studied in relation to an established range—for example, a new colour of paint for the home decorator.

Note on the Word 'Exponential'

Exponential means 'growing (or decaying) at a constant rate' and is used consistently in this sense. However, some confusion may be caused by the fact that it is applied to two different things.

First in exponential (or geometrical) weighting, it describes the set of *weights* by which the individual sales figures are multiplied in order to obtain a weighted average. The weights diminish exponentially in going from one period to its predecessor.

Secondly, as an exponential *trend*, it describes a steady proportional growth (or decay) in the *sales*, regardless of the method by which the growth is measured. Such a growth may equally well be described as a *multiplicative* or *ratio* trend, and the latter term is frequently used here in the hope of reducing the confusion.

Significance of a Regression Coefficient

We have seen that in calculating a linear regression coefficient, we fit a 'best straight line' to a set of points on a graph. Now look at Figure 4.1, which also shows a straight line fitted to a set of points: is it the 'best-fitting' line? (Remember that the goodness-of-fit depends on the sum of the squares of the vertical distances of the individual points from the line, the best fit being obtained when this sum is a minimum.) It is unlikely, since the line was drawn horizontally, and if we allowed it to rotate about a central point, it would give a better fit by taking up a position like that shown in Figure 4.2.

By measuring the extent to which the sum of squares is reduced by such a rotation, a statistician can say whether the regression coefficient is significantly different from zero. The word **significant** is used in a technical sense and is closely allied to the idea of confidence limits discussed on page 31. Like them, it may be assessed at certain levels of risk, usually 5 per cent or less. To say that a regression coefficient is not significant implies that the slope which it describes could have arisen by a chance combination of random effects.

TABLE 4.V

Sales Showing Quadratic Growth

Period	Sales	Trend	Trend of Trend
0	100		
		+5	
1	105		+2
		+7	
2	112		+2
		+9	
3	121		+2
		+11	
4	132		+2
		+13	
5	145		+2
		+15	
6	160		+2
		+17	
7	177		+2
		+19	
8	196		+2
		+21	
9	217		+2
		+23	
10	240		

Quadratic Regression

One way of fitting a curved line to a series of sales figures is, as we have seen, to take logarithms. Another is to fit a **parabola** or **quadratic curve** instead of a straight line. Such a curve is expressed mathematically as

$$s = S + tn + un^2$$

in which s gives the sales in the nth period,
t is the linear trend, and
u is the quadratic trend.

If the base level of sales (S) is 100, t is $+4$ and u is $+1$, we have

In period 1 $s = 100 + 4 + 1 = 105$
In period 2 $s = 100 + 8 + 4 = 112$

and so on.

The sales figures in Table 4.V were generated in this way. Random errors have been kept to zero, so that the behaviour of the trend can be clearly seen: it increases steadily in such a way that the 'trend of the

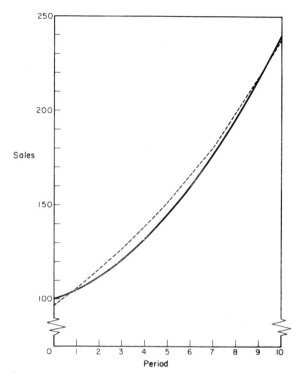

Figure 4.7 Comparison of quadratic (solid line) and logarithmic regression (broken line)

trend' is constant. The curve on which these sales lie is shown in Figure 4.7 as the continuous line.

Quadratic regression may be calculated in the same way as linear regression, except that the set of weights is different.

The broken line in Figure 4.7 enables us to compare the logarithmic and quadratic (or parabolic) curves. It was obtained by calculating the logarithmic regression coefficient for Table 4.IV, which is 0·03914; this is equivalent to a growth rate of 9·43 per cent per annum, and the curve passes through the geometric mean, 152, in period 5.

Exercise 4.9

If the trend of the trend is constant, a parabola will always fit the sales figures perfectly. True or false?

F

Exercise 4.10

If only three sales figures are considered, a quadratic curve will always fit them perfectly. True or false?

Polynomial Regression

If two sales figures will always fit a straight line perfectly, and three fit a quadratic curve perfectly, is there a curve which will always fit four points perfectly? There is: it is called a **cubic**. Its equation contains the cube of n and looks like this:

$$s = S + tn + un^2 + vn^3.$$

One can go on adding terms containing higher powers of n and getting curves which fit closer and closer to a long series of sales figures. Such curves are called **polynomials**, but their use is not advised. They are liable to contain strange kinks and to show sudden changes which cannot be related to any reasonable model of market development.

Take, for example, the following series:

100, 95, 91, 87, 85, 84, 87, 92, 100

This might be interpreted as a slight recession in sales followed by a recovery, but if a cubic equation were fitted, the next five terms would be

110, 123, 141, 162, 188

which would appear (to put it mildly) somewhat over-optimistic.

To sum up, the use of polynomials higher than quadratic is presented rather as a pitfall to be avoided than as a practical method.

Trigonometrical Regression

The yearly rotation of the earth around the sun produces rhythmical variations in intensity of sunlight, temperature, length of day and other variables. The relationship which the time of year bears to these variables closely resembles that which an angle bears to its **sine**. The latter has been calculated and tabulated, and forms the basis of a method of analysing seasonal fluctuations called **sinusoidal regression**.

Since a sine is a trigonometrical function of an angle, the method is more commonly (but less precisely) known as **trigonometrical regression**.

Take Figure 4.8 for example. It shows the mean temperatures at Antwerp throughout the year, and any other place in the temperate zone of the Northern Hemisphere would yield a curve of similar shape. A pure sine curve is shown in Figure 4.9 and it has an obvious resemblance to Figure 4.8.

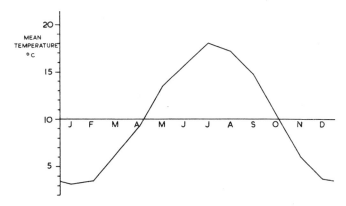

Figure 4.8 Mean temperature in Antwerp

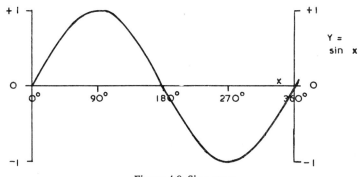

Figure 4.9 Sine curve

Vertical and Horizontal Displacement

One difference between Figures 4.8 and 4.9 is that the former shows a line which oscillates about an average of about 10°C, whereas the latter has a mean zero. Another difference is that the temperature curve agrees with its average value in April and October; the sine curve agrees with its average at what would be January 1st and June 1st if it were on a time scale. This displacement is called the **phase difference**.

As the figures stand, the phase difference cannot be measured because one horizontal scale is in months and the other in degrees. It is not difficult to convert one into the other: a full circle contains 360 degrees and a full year contains 12 months; it follows that 30 degrees are equivalent to one month.

Exercise 4.11

What roughly, is the phase difference in degrees between the curves in Figures 4.8 and 4.9?

Amplitude

The standard sine curve in Figure 4.9 goes from zero to a height of +1, then down through zero to −1 and back again. The height of the curve is called its **amplitude** and is 1 in this case. Note that the amplitude is *half* the distance between the crest of the curve and its trough.

Exercise 4.12

What, roughly, is the amplitude of the curve in Figure 4.8?

Fitting Sine Curves

The method of calculating a trigonometrical regression will not be given here, being beyond the limited mathematical scope of this book. It does not differ in principle from the method of linear regression described earlier: that is to say, the average, amplitude and phase difference are allowed to adjust themselves until the sum of the squares of the deviations is minimized.

Figure 4.10 shows the calculated sine curve superimposed on the actual values of the mean temperature.

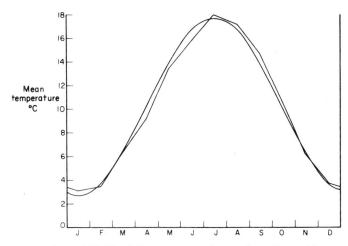

Figure 4.10 Fitted sine curve superimposed on Figure 4.8

Products whose sales depend upon the ambient temperature, including those listed in Table 2.V (page 36) as well as other fuels, may be dealt with in this way.

An analysis for heating oil is given in Figure 4.11: in this, linear and sinusoidal trends have both been extracted. Heating oil is, in fact, the 'commodity' in Table 1.I, and the 'total sales' in Figure 4.11 agree with the sales given in that table.

Multiple Regression

So far we have considered only those cases in which sales depend upon time. Time is called the **independent variable** and sales are the **dependent variable**. Sales may, however, be forecast from two or more independent variables. For instance, the demand for cement may be dictated by the forecast levels of activity in four different sorts of construction: residential, non-residential, roads and other. Another example is sales of motor spirit from a service station, which may be affected by traffic density, accessibility (a difficult thing to measure), the average waiting time and so on.

A common pair of independent variables is time and temperature, and weather forecasts are consulted in forecasting the demand for fuels and for foods such as ice cream and soft drinks. For example, there

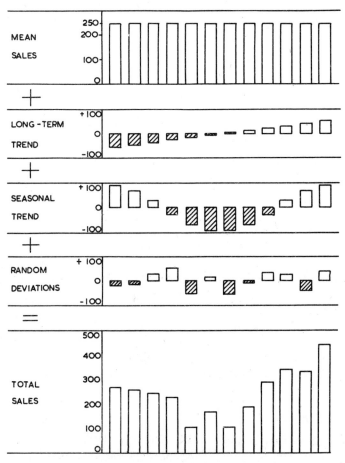

Figure 4.11 Monthly sales of heating oil—analysis

is a rule of thumb in the gas industry that the demand for gas in any one day will change by about 1 per cent for every degree Fahrenheit by which the temperature differs from a standardized value of 60°F. This is part of the so-called Degree Day system.

Multiple regression is a method which may be used in such cases. As in all other methods of regression, it is calculated by minimizing the sum of squares of deviations, but these are from a surface instead of a line.

There will be as many regression coefficients as there are independent variables, and each may be tested for significance against the residual error.

Like trigonometrical regression, multiple regression will almost certainly need to be calculated by an electronic computer, and standard programs for doing so are available.

Correlation

We saw in Chapter 1 that two variables may be correlated even though one does not depend upon the other. The extent to which they do so may be calculated as a **correlation coefficient**, which in turn may be tested for significance.

It cannot be too strongly emphasized that a significant correlation does not imply a cause and effect. Statisticians delight in collecting 'nonsense correlations': births correlated with the number of storks sighted, or priests ordained in New York with output of cars in Detroit. Nigel Balchin in *The Small Back Room* (Collins) describes the analysis of a test on rifle bullets:

Till said, 'There's an extraordinary thing here, Sammy.'
'What?' I said. I knew Till's extraordinary things.
'You know those penetration figures?'
'Mm.'
'Well, there's a positive correlation between penetration and the height of the man firing.'
'Easy,' I said. 'The taller the man, the more rarefied the atmosphere and the less the air resistance.'
'You think that might be it?' said Till, putting his spectacles down and blinking.
'Might be?' I said. 'It's obvious. At least it would be if they hadn't all been lying down when they fired. As it was, I suppose the longer chaps were nearer the target. How the hell did you get their heights anyhow?'
'I thought they might be interesting,' said Till vaguely. 'But if they were lying down, it's very puzzling isn't it?'
'What is the correlation?' I said. 'About 0·01?'
'Oh no,' said Till, hurt. 'It's about 0·09.'
'Well, that's lower than the correlation you got between Roman Catholicism and weight lifting ability, so I wouldn't worry too much about it.'
Till shook his head. He wasn't satisfied. He never was satisfied.

When Till spoke of a positive correlation, he meant that the penetration *increased* as the height of the man increased. On the other hand, sales of bread and cake are apt to be *negatively* correlated, since the one increases as the other decreases. In any case, Till's correlation coefficient of 0·09 would certainly not be significant.

Turning to a more serious example, one may quote a large international company in which the increase in sales during a year was significantly correlated with the number of new territories opened. In the absence of any other evidence, we may surmise that

(*a*) the new territories were entered because the company found enough money coming in to do so;

(*b*) entering the new territories generated the extra sales (so soon?);

(*c*) both things happened in a general atmosphere of prosperity.

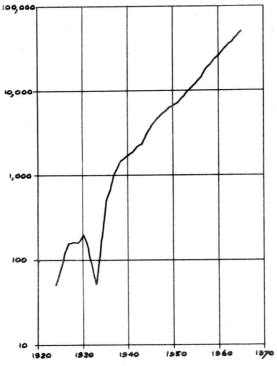

Figure 4.12 A. C. Nielsen Co.: Consolidated sales 1924–64 in thousands of dollars

The last of these is a frequent explanation of correlation, in that both variables are changing because of a common cause.

The direct usefulness of correlation, then, is usually slight. If there is no significant correlation between two variables, there can be no significant regression of one on the other. On the other hand, if they *are* correlated, a regression cannot be assumed without further evidence, and the correlation coefficient itself cannot be used to derive the value of one variable from that of another.

A Case Study in Regression Analysis

Table 4.VI shows the consolidated sales of the A. C. Nielsen Company, the world's largest marketing research organization, since its foundation in 1924, and Figure 4.12 is a graph of the sales against

TABLE 4.VI

A. C. Nielsen Company
Consolidated Sales by Fiscal Year, 1924–1964
(Expressed in U.S. dollars)

Fiscal Year	Consolidated Sales	Fiscal Year	Consolidated Sales
1924	52,081	1945	4,509,134
25	80,309	46	5,124,959
26	125,773	47	5,813,552
27	161,652	48	6,539,936
28	165,396	49	6,767,116
29	163,331	1950	7,353,536
1930	205,854	51	8,488,107
31	164,823	52	9,894,691
32	97,155	53	10,974,698
33	52,039	54	12,322,026
34	156,020	55	14,377,440
35	472,096	56	17,952,348
36	656,817	57	20,822,568
37	1,014,756	58	24,132,259
38	1,440,050	59	26,858,133
39	1,745,660	1960	31,019,342
1940	1,914,992	61	36,162,495
41	2,203,427	62	40,119,321
42	2,341,774	63	45,348,981
43	3,056,826	64	50,588,408
44	3,707,710		

time, on four-cycle semi-logarithmic paper. The company's early
vicissitudes are clearly shown, as is its sustained and rapid growth in
more recent years. As a demonstration of the use of regression analysis,
we shall forecast, from the data for the five years 1956–1960 inclusive,
the sales over the next four years, and also calculate their average rate
of growth. First, the numbers of the years are simplified, thus:

$$
\left.
\begin{array}{r}
1956 \rightarrow -2 \\
1957 \rightarrow -1 \\
(\text{average}) \quad 1958 \rightarrow 0 \\
1959 \rightarrow +1 \\
1960 \rightarrow +2
\end{array}
\right\}
\begin{array}{l}
\text{Sum of squares,} \\
10
\end{array}
$$

Next, the sales are transformed in two stages: (a) they are expressed in
units of one million dollars; (b) the resultant figures are then converted
into their logarithms.

$$
\begin{array}{r}
17 \cdot 952 \rightarrow 1 \cdot 25407 \\
20 \cdot 823 \rightarrow 1 \cdot 31849 \\
24 \cdot 132 \rightarrow 1 \cdot 38255 \\
26 \cdot 858 \rightarrow 1 \cdot 42911 \\
31 \cdot 019 \rightarrow 1 \cdot 49164 \\
\hline
\end{array}
$$

Total	6·87586
Average	1·37517

Then the two sets of figures are multiplied together and the products
totalled:

Year	Log Sales	Product
−2	1·25407	−2·50814
−1	1·31849	−1·31849
0	1·38255	0
+1	1·42911	+1·42911
+2	1·49164	+2·98328
	Total	+0·58576

The slope of the regression line is calculated as $+0 \cdot 58576/10 =
+0 \cdot 05858$.

Working from the average 1·37517 in 1958, we have as projected
values:

1961 $1 \cdot 37517 + 3 \times 0 \cdot 05858 = 1 \cdot 55091$
1962 $1 \cdot 55091 + 0 \cdot 05858 \quad = 1 \cdot 60949$
1963 $1 \cdot 60949 + 0 \cdot 05858 \quad = 1 \cdot 66807$
1964 $1 \cdot 66807 + 0 \cdot 05858 \quad = 1 \cdot 72665$

All that remains is to transform the figures in the last column into their antilogarithms and then multiply by a million to give

1961   35,555,000
1962   40,690,000
1963   46,570,000
1964   53,284,000.

The 95 per cent confidence limits may also be calculated by the method described on page 31. Table 4.VII gives these limits as well as the forecasts, and also includes the actual sales for comparison.

TABLE 4.VII

Year	Forecast sales	95% Confidence limits		Actual sales
		Lower	Upper	
1961	35,555,000	34,682,000	36,451,000	36,162,495
1962	40,690,000	39,400,000	42,025,000	40,119,321
1963	46,570,000	44,781,000	48,428,000	45,348,981
1964	53,284,000	50,874,000	55,834,000	50,588,408

Rate of Growth

The antilogarithm of $0 \cdot 05858$ is $1 \cdot 144$ and hence the rate of growth may be expressed as $+ 14 \cdot 4$ per cent per annum.

The period in which sales would be expected to double, obtained by dividing log 2 ($0 \cdot 30103$) by $0 \cdot 05858$, is $5 \cdot 2$ years, assuming that growth will continue at $14 \cdot 4$ per cent.

5 SEASONAL EFFECTS

Some ways of estimating seasonal effects have already been outlined. Yet another method exists, based on a statistical method called **analysis of variance**. (This is not to be confused with the quite different technique of the same name, used by cost accountants.) It has an advantage over trigonometrical regression in that it does not require us to assume that seasonal effects are related by a sine curve. Its disadvantage is that it needs two years' figures at least, whereas trigonometrical regression can be worked out from those for one year only.

The method will be illustrated by a study which is a slightly simplified version of a case from real life. As well as demonstrating the forecasting method, it will show how stock control based on residual errors may be incorporated.

Case Study in Seasonal Forecasting and Stock Control

The Classic Sportswear Company makes a standard type of sports shirt; there is a demand for it all the year round but the sales reach a peak in the summer. In spite of changes in style to keep it in fashion, sales have tended to decline slowly; for the last three years the annual figures have been:

1960	15,932
1961	14,421
1962	14,406

No one feels very sure about the future trend: the sales level may settle down at about 14,000, although the market research department hopes that the new design will give a boost to demand. On the whole, the sales manager tends towards pessimism, and takes the view that the sales for 1963 are not likely to exceed 13,200.

Orders for replenishment are placed on the factory and fortunately there is no particular need to smooth the manufacturing load. However, studies of economic lot sizes [6] have been made, in collaboration with the production manager; they have led to a decision to aim at placing the orders for replenishment at regular intervals of three months.

The sales for the previous month are known in the first week of the current month, and an order placed immediately will be delivered in two months' time—that is, just before the end of the month following.

The problem is now reduced to two questions: At what level of stock should an order be placed? How much should be ordered?

Sales Analysis

The sales analysis is given in Table 5.I, which contains the monthly sales for the last three years. The total annual sales and average monthly sales in each year are seen as the column totals and means for 1960, 1961 and 1962. The overall monthly mean for the last three years, 1,243, is seen at the foot of the second-last column.

The rows are totalled and averaged, and the average sales over the past three years are obtained for each month, e.g. 544 for January. The overall average, 1,243, is subtracted from each of these to give the 'seasonal trend' figure in the last column. For January, $544 - 1,243 = -699$, the negative sign showing that sales for that month are below the year round average. The total seasonal trend is of course zero, except for a small rounding error of $+4$.

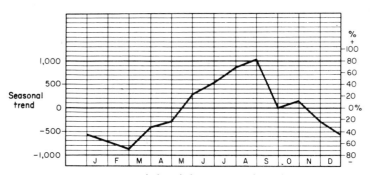

Figure 5.1 'Classic' shirts: seasonal trend

Figure 5·1 shows the trend graphically, both in numbers of shirts on the left hand scale and as a percentage above or below the average monthly figure on the right-hand scale. The range of seasonal variation is high—high enough to make early detection of long-term trends difficult and to introduce complications into the regulation of stocks.

Sales Forecasting

The next step is to forecast the monthly sales for 1963. The total annual sales have already been forecast as 13,200, giving a monthly average of 1,100. It is only necessary to add the latter to the seasonal trends in the last column of Tables 5.I to obtain the individual monthly

TABLE 5.I
Monthly Sales of Sports Shirts

Month	1960	1961	1962	Total	Mean	Seasonal effects
January	371	437	825	1,633	544	− 699
February	470	445	329	1,244	415	− 828
March	534	1,434	512	2,480	827	− 416
April	1,556	768	576	2,900	967	− 276
May	1,238	2,052	1,332	4,622	1,541	+ 298
June	2,266	1,268	1,784	5,318	1,773	+ 530
July	2,722	1,231	2,417	6,370	2,123	+ 880
August	2,494	2,430	2,016	6,940	2,313	+ 1070
September	1,202	1,311	1,309	3,822	1,274	+ 31
October	1,374	1,300	1,616	4,290	1,430	+ 187
November	1,016	900	1,094	3,010	1,003	− 240
December	689	845	596	2,130	710	− 533
Total	15,932	14,421	14,406	44,759	—	(+ 4)
Mean	1,328	1,202	1,200	—	1,243	

forecasts for 1963. They are given together with their cumulative totals, in Table 5.II.

TABLE 5.II
Forecast Monthly Sales for 1963

Month	Sales	Cumulative sales
January	401	401
February	272	673
March	684	1,357
April	824	2,181
May	1,398	3,579
June	1,630	5,209
July	1,980	7,189
August	2,170	9,359
September	1,131	10,490
October	1,287	11,777
November	860	12,637
December	567	13,204
Total	13,204	
Mean	1,100	

Random Errors

If the seasonal effects and averages for each year were the only factors governing the individual monthly sales figures, the latter would be as shown in Table 5.III. These interpolated values were obtained by adding the year's average to the seasonal effect. For example, for January 1960,

$$1,328 + (-699) = 629.$$

TABLE 5.III

Interpolated Values

1960	1961	1962	Seasonal effects
629	503	501	− 699
500	374	372	− 828
912	786	784	− 416
1,052	926	924	− 276
1,626	1,500	1,498	+ 298
1,858	1,732	1,730	+ 530
2,208	2,082	2,080	+ 880
2,398	2,272	2,270	+ 1,070
1,359	1,233	1,231	+ 31
1,515	1,389	1,387	+ 187
1,088	962	960	− 240
795	669	667	− 533

Monthly Averages	1,328	1,202	1,200

The differences between the figures in Table 5.III and those in Table 5.I are the random errors, and they are given individually in Table 5.IV, and grouped in Table 5.V. The latter is shown as a barchart in Figure 5.2.

The standard deviation calculated from the random errors is 407, so the 95 per cent confidence limits of a forecast for one month ahead are about ±800. This means that a buffer stock of 800 items will be needed to cover errors in the forecast for one month ahead, the risk level being a little greater than 2·5 per cent.

It cannot be too strongly emphasized that this figure of 2·5 per cent was discussed with the sales manager. He would naturally have preferred a better level of customer service, but agreed to this compromise

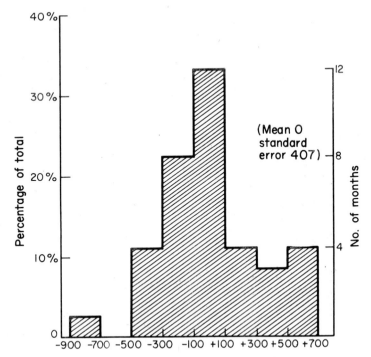

Figure 5.2 'Classic' shirts: bar-chart of errors

TABLE 5.IV

Random Errors

	1960	1961	1962
January	− 258	− 66	+ 324
February	− 30	+ 71	− 43
March	− 378	+ 648	− 272
April	+ 504	− 158	− 348
May	− 388	+ 552	− 166
June	+ 408	− 464	+ 54
July	+ 514	− 851	+ 337
August	+ 96	+ 158	− 254
September	− 157	+ 78	+ 78
October	− 141	− 89	+ 229
November	− 72	− 62	+ 134
December	− 106	+ 176	− 71

TABLE 5.V

Random Elements in Monthly Sales Figures 1960–62

Range	Frequency No. of months	%
− 900 to − 701	1	2·7
− 700 to − 501	0	0
− 500 to − 301	4	11·1
− 300 to − 101	8	22·2
− 100 to + 99	12	33·3
+ 100 to + 299	4	11·1
+ 300 to + 499	3	8·3
+ 500 to + 699	4	11·1
Total	36	99·8

figure after studying the increased demand for working capital which higher stocks would have engendered. To make such a decision is hard; what is even harder is to stick to it when the one in forty chance turns up.

Buffer Stock

800 items would be the appropriate buffer stock for a period of one month, but the lead time is in fact two months. Do we then need 1,600 items? The answer is no; because for the error to exceed 800 items in two *successive* months would be most unlikely. (It would occur only once in 1,600 times.) In order to allow for the 'swings and-round-abouts' effect, statisticians tell us that we must multiply the 800 not by two but by its square root. This is 1·414, so we get $(1·414 \times 800) =$ 1,131 as the buffer stock for a two-month period. Similarly, for a three-month period we multiply by 1·732, the square root of three.

Re-ordering Levels

The next stage is to deduce the re-ordering level (ROL) by adding the expected sales during the lead time to the buffer stock, but since the sales vary seasonally, the expected sales will depend upon the time of year. At the end of January, the expected sales will be the total for February and March, i.e. 272 + 684 = 956; adding 1,131 buffer stock gives the ROL for the end of January as 2,087. The complete set of

G

ROLs calculated in this way is given in Table 5.VI, and drawn as the peaked control line in Figure 5.3.

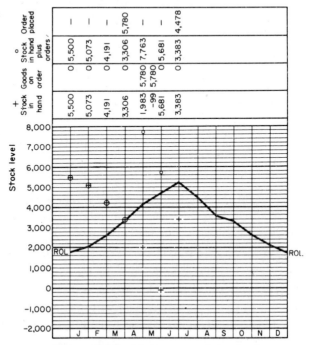

Figure 5.3 'Classic' shirts: re-ordering levels

An order placed at the end of January will be received at the end of March, and used up during April, May and June. The total expected sales during these three months are

$$824 + 1,398 + 1,630 = 3,852$$

which can be found in Table 5.VI as the ROQ for the end of January. The rest are calculated similarly.

Stock Control Chart

The two questions 'when?' and 'how much?' have now been answered, by the tabulated ROL and ROQ respectively. Figure 5.3 shows the stock control chart which is used for applying these figures.

At the top of the chart, the total stock, both in hand and on order, is compiled and then plotted on the grid below. As long as it is above the ROL line no action is necessary. By the end of February, the stock is approaching the ROL and will be subjected to frequent 'spot checks' during March; it crosses the ROL just before the end of March, and so replenishments are ordered; Table 5.VI gives the number to be ordered as 5,780.

TABLE 5.VI
Monthly Values of ROL and ROQ

Month	ROL	ROQ
January	2,087	3,852
February	2,639	5,008
March	3,353	5,780
April	4,159	5,281
May	4,741	4,588
June	5,281	3,278
July	4,432	2,714
August	3,549	1,828
September	3,278	1,240
October	2,558	1,357
November	2,099	1,780
December	1,804	2,906
Average	3,331	3,300

The sales manager has the option of delegating the authority to re-order, or he may ask to be notified first; the system can deal with either case.

The order comes in just before the end of May and is added to the stock. Just before it comes in, the stock runs out, and a small backlog of 99 items is built up. Was this due to an exceptionally large random element, or to a change in either the seasonal or long-term trend? The sales control chart provides an answer.

The limits of random fluctuation have already been chosen as ±800 in any one month, from which ±1,131 was deduced for two months. Similarly, for three months we calculate the limits as ±1,386, and so on. This gives the limits for the cumulative sales throughout the year, tabulated in Tables 5.VII and shown as the diagonal control lines in the sales control chart, Figure 5.4; the curvature of these lines is caused by the allowance they make for the seasonal trend. The cumulative sales are plotted on the chart, and we know that as long as they stay within the limits, there have been no changes of any significance in the sales

TABLE 5.VII
TABLE 5.VII

Sales Control Chart Limits

Month	Multiplier (sq. root)	Limits	Control lines Lower	Control lines Upper
January	1·000	± 800	—	1,201
February	1·414	± 1,131	—	1,804
March	1·732	± 1,386	—	2,743
April	2·000	± 1,600	581	3,781
May	2·236	± 1,789	1,790	5,368
June	2·449	± 1,959	3,250	7,168
July	2·646	± 2,117	5,072	9,306
August	2·828	± 2,262	7,970	11,611
September	3·000	± 2,400	8,090	12,890
October	3·162	± 2,530	9,247	14,307
November	3·317	± 2,654	9,983	15,291
December	3·464	± 2,771	10,443	15,975
For current MAT	14,406	± 2,771	11,635	17,177

trends. If a point falls outside the limits, either the seasonal or the long-term trend will have altered.

To find out which, we add a pair of control lines for the moving annual total, using the 12-month limits. They are seen to slope slightly downwards in the chart, reflecting the forecast drop in sales from the current annual total, 14,406, to the forecast total of 13,200 for 1963. If a point falls outside these limits, the long-term trend must have changed.

The backlog of orders shown on the stock control chart occurred towards the end of May. The MAT plot at that time shows that no significant change has taken place in the long-term trend, although the point is very near the upper limit. The cumulative figure is above the limit, indicating abnormally high seasonal sales, and this leads to the charts being brought to the sales manager. He concludes that his pessimistic estimate may well have been wrong, and asks for weekly reports on the situation. By the middle of June, the stock has fallen below the ROL, and at the end of June the upward trend in sales has been definitely indicated.

The sales manager must now make a new forecast of the sales, and decides that 18,000 is now a more likely figure for the year ahead. In reaching this decision, he uses the control chart as only one small piece of evidence: mostly he relies on his skill in interpreting the reports of

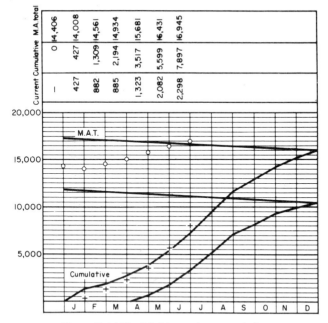

Figure 5.4 'Classic' shirts: sales control chart

his representatives, in detecting the 'feel' of the market and in using an upward turn in sales as a means of justifying an increase in his advertising budget.

Control Action

The new prediction is an increase of 400 a month on the previous estimate, so the ROQ (three months' sales) is immediately adjusted:

$$3,278 + 3 \times 400 = 4,478$$

The ROL is also temporarily raised by $2 \times 400 = 800$ for the rest of the year, pending the preparation of a revised chart. The increase in sales has been detected with no undue delay, and corrected smoothly and efficiently; the sales manager's work has been directed solely towards essential decisions, uncluttered by routine.

At the beginning of the year, Classic Sportswear can predict very closely with this system what their expected average stock will be.

It is equal to half the average ROQ ($\frac{1}{2} \times 3,300 = 1,650$) plus the two months' buffer stock, 1,131, that is 2,781. The maximum stock, on the other hand, is found by adding the buffer stock to the maximum ROQ, i.e. $1,131 + 5,780 = 6,911$. Classic can also predict that the maximum stock will probably be reached in May, anticipating the holiday peak. This is only an estimate, and as it turned out, the maximum was rather higher and also earlier.

Recapitulation

We can see a chain of events at work here which has important implications for policy-making. The initial sales prediction for the year as a whole was a single figure for which the sales manager bore the responsibility; an exhaustive statistical analysis of the previous three years enabled his advisers (or a computer) to translate this into a detailed forward plan and a simple graphical control system. This in turn, by taking into account the reasonable range of error in the forecasts, gave early warning of an improvement in sales. From this followed a quick, almost mechanical adaptation of the control system to the new conditions.

Finally, the statistical analysis provided a basis for making a further set of forecasts relating to working capital, and the whole operation called for close collaboration between the sales, production and accounting functions. It was, indeed, a step towards what is sometimes called the 'total systems' approach to management.

Exercise 5.1

Read through the case carefully and try to decide at what points the sales manager was called upon to exercise his managerial judgment as distinct from participating in routine.

Exercise 5.2

A breakdown in the works of Classic's main supplier sends the lead time up to three months. How would the system be affected?

Exercise 5.3

The company's accountant values the stock at four shillings per shirt. How much extra working capital would be needed if the lead time went up from two months to three?

6 MARKET SATURATION

When we fit a simple trend, be it linear, quadratic, or multiplicative, we usually imply a limited period of validity: somewhere in the back of his mind the sales manager says: 'But it cannot go on for ever like this.' Such a case arose when we considered the linear downward trend in 78 rpm gramophone records; another is exemplified in Table 6.I.

TABLE 6.I
Imports of Motor-Cycles from Japan to U.K.

Year	Number
1960	465
1961	1,725
1962	4,270
1963	51,600

(Source: *The Times*, 22 June 1965, p.15.)

Assuming a constant ratio trend and applying linear regression to the logarithms of the sales as described in Chapter 4, we get the following statistics:

Mean of logarithms 3·562; geometric mean 3,650
Regression coefficient of logarithms + 0·653
Antilog   4·50

So the imports for each year tend to be four-and-a-half times as great as those for the preceding year, and the forecast for 1964 is

$$\text{Antilog } (3·562 + 2·5 \times 0·653) = 156,300$$

The growth of these imports is shown plotted on 3-cycle semi-log paper in Figure 6.1 (*overleaf*).

The rate of increase is so great, and its implications for British manufacturers so unpleasant, that one may decide to take refuge in the comforting assumption of market saturation.

I happen to know nothing about the potential market for Japanese motor-cycles in Britain, but I am going to pretend that after much consultation with economists and market researchers, a saturation figure of 200,000 a year is adopted as the best available estimate. It is important to note that this is a limiting *rate* of consumption, not a cumulative *total*. Our assumption about the market is now changed. There is still a gap of 148,400 but it will be filled by an annual increase in sales every year, the trend in fact. In any one year, the trend will be only two-thirds or 67 per cent of that in the previous year.

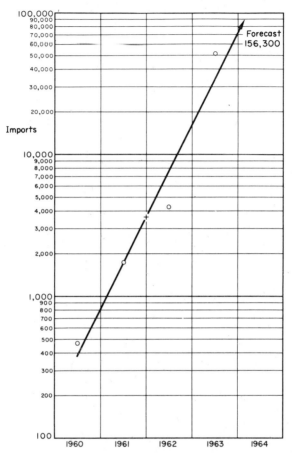

Figure 6.1 Imports of motor-cycles from Japan to U.K.

Modified Exponential Trend

Now we have to find out what these annual increments will be. If the increase in the first year is t, that in the following year will be $0{\cdot}67t$, then $(0{\cdot}67)^2t$ and so on. After an infinitely long time, the gap would be completely filled, so

$$148{,}400 = t + 0{\cdot}67t + (0{\cdot}67)^2t + (0{\cdot}67)^3t + \ldots$$

This looks a difficult equation to solve because there is an infinite number of terms on the right-hand side. In fact, as so often happens with exponentials, it turns out to be quite easy. One can prove mathematically that the right-hand side adds up to

$$\frac{t}{1-0\cdot67} \text{ which equals } 3t$$

$$\text{so } t = \frac{148,400}{3} = 49,500$$

We now know the increase in sales over the base year (which we have taken as 1963) during the following year. The next increase will be two-thirds of this, 33,000, and so on. Table 6.II, which shows the forecast growth over the next few years, is built up by continuing this procedure.

The gradually decreasing trend is shown in Fig. 6.2. It is an upsidedown version of the ordinary exponential curve, and is called the modified exponential.

(The mathematical equation for this curve is

$$s = M - (M - S)r^n$$

in which s represents the sales in period n,
M represents the sales at market saturation,
r is the common ratio and must be less than 1, and
S is the initial sales level.)

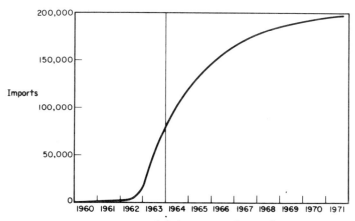

Figure 6.2 Modified exponential growth

Revising the Assumptions

The forecast for 1964 would have been 156,300 if the exponential growth of 1960–1963 had continued unchecked. As it turned out, the actual imports in 1964 were 99,208. Were the new assumptions justified, and should we continue with them?

The short answer is that we still have very little evidence one way or the other. Although the actual figure was only about two-thirds of the old 'exponential growth' forecast (156,300), the difference between their logarithms is 0·197. The standard deviation of the individual points about the line is 0·186, so the actual imports would fall well within the confidence limits of the 'old' forecast for 1964.

There are limits to what we can assess with our eyes alone. Psychologists know that our perception of what we see is conditioned by what we *want* to see, and the dispassionate calculations of a statistician provide a useful counter to the personal bias which may affect our reading of curves or tables.

TABLE 6.II

Forecast Imports of Motor-cycles from Japan

Year	Forecast increase on previous year	Forecast total
1963	(Base year)	(51,600 actual)
1964	+49,500	101,100
1965	+33,000	134,100
1966	+22,000	156,100
1967	+14,700	170,800
1968	+9,800	180,600
1969	+6,500	187,100
1970	+4,300	191,400

Yet another danger lurks: we made *two* assumptions when we began with, first, a market estimate of 200,000 and secondly, a decay factor of 67 per cent. Other pairs of figures could give similar results, and the need for constant review is obvious.

There may even be a case for simple *linear* regression during the transition from the exponential to the modified exponential curve.

Exercise 6.1

Produce a table of forecasts similar to Table 6.II, but based on the following new assumptions:

Market saturation will be achieved at 500,000 a year.

The increase in imports in any year will be 90 per cent of that in the previous year.

(To make the calculation easier, round off the 1963 figure to 50,000.)

Exercise 6.2

Suppose that we know the actual imports for 1964 as well as the figures in Table 6.I, and we assume that their growth will be linear during the years 1963 to 1966 inclusive. Forecast the imports for 1965 and 1966.

Growth in Nature

The growth of sales and their decline may be viewed as natural phenomena, and some attempts have been made to relate the behaviour of a market to that of other populations.

The general theory is that an increase in population causes an increasing demand on limited resources such as food. Then each individual has a decreasing share and this checks the growth of the population. (In sales terms, the 'resource' to be competed for is the total market capacity and the individual items sold make up the total 'population' which is competing for it.)

The most widely known theory in this field was put forward by Malthus in 1798. The population, he said, was increasing exponentially, but the supply of food was only growing arithmetically: therefore he predicted widespread famine. Malthus may well turn out to have been right in the long run: the population *is* growing exponentially, and food supplies are not keeping up with it. Nevertheless, his prediction of arithmetical increase, that is to say, of a constant additive trend, was too pessimistic. He failed to foresee the great advances in methods of food production such as long-range fishing and artificial fertilizers. There is a lesson in this for the over-cautious forecaster.

Pearl's Law

Pearl's Law describes a growth which is rapid at first, but then begins to fall off and flatten out. It is expressed as a mathematical equation

$$s = 1/(p + qr^n), \text{ with } p \text{ and } q \text{ constant}$$

of which the graph has the shape shown in Figure 6.3. This particular curve is called a **logistic** curve, and is one of a general category called **sigmoid** because they have the shape of a flattened 'S'.

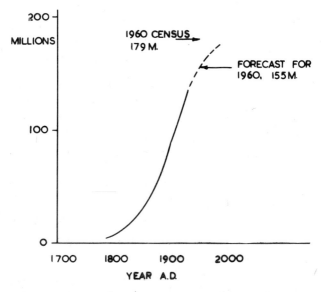

Figure 6.3 Logistic curve for population of United States of America, 1790 to 1940. (Adapted from Pearl, R., Reed, L. J., and Keith, J. F., in *Science*, 1940, **93**, p. 486)

Pearl, by the way, made his observations on fruit flies confined in a jar; this is an example of a biological model as distinct from the mathematical one derived from it. (To what extent, we may ask, is it a valid model of the consumer population?)

The example in Figure 6.3 is seen to be pessimistic, as so many sigmoid extrapolations are. Population data for 150 years, projected only 20 years into the future, gave an estimate of 155 millions for the population of the United States in 1960. The actual population in that year was 179 millions, a level which the projected logistic curve did not reach until A.D. 2020.

Gompertz and Other Curves

There is another commonly-used sigmoid curve called the Gompertz curve (its equation is $\log s = p + qr^n$: r must lie between zero and 1 in this as in the logistic and modified exponential curves). In general, a variety of sigmoids can be constructed by combining two terms which represent growth and decay. To fit such curves is very much a matter for the professional statistician: those who may be interested can find much detail in an excellent I.C.I. monograph. [11]

The Christmas Rush

Sigmoid curves are usually associated with long-term projections, but they can be made useful in some short-term manipulations. Many companies manufacture special items for one season—fashion goods for summer or a Christmas gift pack—which will have little or no value once the season is over. A typical sales curve for such goods is shown in Figure 6.4 (*a*); for the sake of simplicity the total number sold is made equal to 100, but this number may also be interpreted as a percentage of any other total. (Note that the curve may be obtained by analysing the behaviour of previous similar lines in much the same way as Tables 5.I and 5.II.) The cumulative sales are shown by the curve in Figure 6.4 (*b*). From this we can read, for example, that half the expected total sales should have been achieved by the end of Week 46.

The Sales-Proportional Scale

The key to the cumulative sales method lies in adjusting the horizontal time scale in such a way that the sigmoid curve in Figure 6.4 (*b*) is distorted into a straight line. The reason is that straight lines can be more easily extrapolated by eye than curved ones.

The result is shown in Figure 6.5. The horizontal distance corresponding to each week has been drawn proportional to the expected sales in that week. (In this case, the scale has been specially drawn, but sometimes a standard paper like arithmetic probability paper can be used.)

The simple diagonal graph has been elaborated into quite a sophisticated control chart. Two converging 'confidence limits' or 'action limits' have been drawn: they may be the product either of the sales

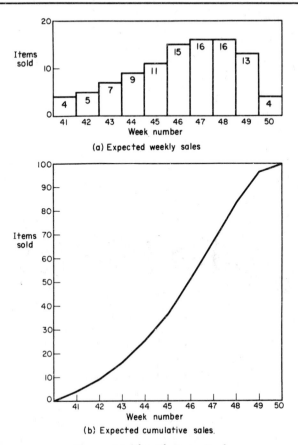

(a) Expected weekly sales

(b) Expected cumulative sales.

Figure 6.4 The Christmas Rush

manager's experience or of statistical analysis as for Tables 5.VII (see page 88).

Two contingencies have also been covered. If sales are well above the expected level they will fall above the action limit and into the shaded area labelled 'emergency production'. However, the chart also shows that this option ceases at the end of Week 46, after which it would be too late anyway.

If sales are too low, a policy of wait-and-see is to be followed until the end of Week 46, after which efforts will be made to boost the sales by reducing the price.

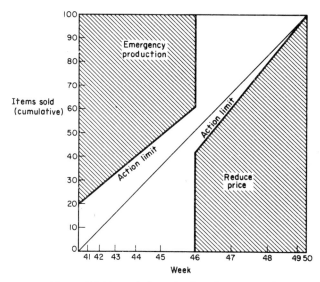

Figure 6.5 Control chart for the Christmas rush

With such a control chart, the sales manager can delegate his supervision of each item during the hectic period of the Christmas rush. A quick glance at the chart will keep him well-informed of progress, and he may still be required to use his discretion, as the next exercise shows.

Exercise 6.3

In the first few weeks of the Christmas rush, the weekly sales have been

Week	(a)	(b)	(c)
41	20	5	0
42	0	4	5
43	5	2	15
44	10	1	16

What would you expect the sales manager to do in each of these situations?

A Case Study in Long-Term Forecasting

Whitting has recently described a case of long-term forecasting for the Central Electricity Generating Board. [7] The first step is to define the objective, which is 'to develop and maintain an efficient, co-ordinated and economical system of supply of electricity in bulk for all parts of England and Wales'. Because of the high rate of growth of demand, the impossibility of storage and the fact that it takes five or more years to build a power station, the forecast needs to be made for at least six years ahead. The definition of data is of some importance; in an earlier example we looked at the actual *units* of electricity distributed and projections of this figure may be of interest in estimating, say, fuel requirements. In forecasts of generating capacity, the impossibility of storage dictates the use of *maximum demand* instead.

Studies of uncertainty are important in deciding what reserve margins of capacity are to be provided. Whitting lists three main sources of uncertainty: in estimates of maximum demand during an average cold spell, in weather and in the availability of plant. Each has been studied in detail, and the distribution of their errors is known. The latter are combined to give a single distribution of the Plant–Load margins: it turns out that a margin of nearly 14 per cent above the estimated demand in an average cold spell is needed if the probability of failure to meet demand is to be negligibly small.

In projecting trends in maximum demand, eleven types of curve were tried. The results are shown in Figure 6.6. [7]

The narrowness of the band containing curves *e* to *k* is worthy of note, since this group of functions contains the linear–exponential (a steady rate of growth) and the two sigmoid curves.

> All these curves fit the past data well enough to be practically indistinguishable on a diagram. Many of these S-shaped curves tend to an exponential curve as certain of the parameters tend to infinity, and it is of interest that great difficulty was experienced in fitting them due to these parameters becoming very large. Since the exponential curve is the simplest to consider, and its extrapolation lies within the limits of the curves examined, it was selected for further study. (Ref. [7], p. 110)

Here, then, is an example of assumptions being examined and revised as shown in Figure 1.4.

After the overall need for new plant has been obtained from the forecast, further decisions about types of plant need to be taken. Low-capital/high-fuel-cost plants deal with the peaks, while high-capital/low-fuel-cost plants meet the base load, but the problem is to find the most suitable mix of the various types available. Forecasts of the

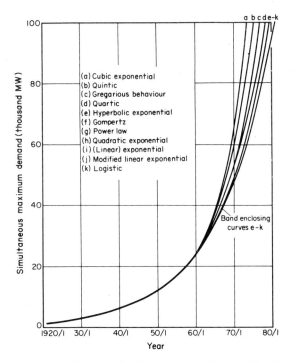

Figure 6.6 Growth curves fitted to maximum demand for electricity

production costs for several alternatives are obtained by simulating their operation on an electronic computer. This in turn leads to questions about siting new power stations, at which stage the transportation method of linear programming is used as an aid to minimizing costs of transporting fuel and distributing electricity.

Conclusion

So we end where we began, with forecast, decision and action intertwined and inseparable. A re-reading of Chapter 1 would now be a profitable exercise.

The essentially simple methods described in this book can be made even simpler by short-cut methods which statisticians have devised: I have preferred to go the long way round so that the reason for the calculations was not concealed by their elegance.

H

The control charts described here are only samples; they can (and should) be modified and adapted to suit the circumstances of any special business or department.

If you feel like following any of the methods outlined here, remember that in the early stages it is as well to have a 'driving instructor' available in the person of a professional statistician. A big company will probably stand the expense of management consultants, but the smaller organization may be able to find enthusiastic (and surprisingly cheap) help from the nearest technical college or university. But watch out in any case for the 'witch-doctors' who keep telling you how difficult it all is (and therefore, how clever they must be). If a man cannot tell you in simple language what he is doing and why, then he probably does not understand it himself.

APPENDIX **LOGARITHMS**

Simple arithmetic starts with $1+1=2$.
Simple logarithms start with $10 \times 10 = 100$.
Two tens multiplied together make 100: we write this fact in the following way:

$$10^2 = 100.$$

Or we can put it another way: how many tens must we multiply together to get 100? The answer is 2, which is called the **logarithm** of 100 to **base** 10. This relationship is written as

$$2 = \log_{10} 100.$$

Scientists sometimes use bases other than 10, but these need not concern us here. It is usually taken for granted that base 10 is being used, so we simply write:

$$2 = \log 100.$$

Exercise A.1

What are the logarithms of
(a) 1,000?
(b) 1,000,000?
(c) 10?

For numbers which consist of 1 followed only by zeros (and with no decimal point) the logarithm is the same as the number of zeros.

Exercise A.2

What numbers have the following logarithms?
(a) 5?
(b) 12?
(c) 0?

Now suppose that we multiply 100 by 1,000:

$$100 = 10 \times 10 \qquad = 10^2 \text{ or log} \qquad 100 = 2$$
$$1,000 = 10 \times 10 \times 10 = 10^3 \text{ or log} \qquad 1,000 = 3$$
$$100 \times 1,000 = 10^2 \times 10^3 \qquad = 10^5 \text{ or log } 100,000 = 5$$

Then multiplying two numbers is equivalent to adding their logarithms, since $2+3=5$.

Exercise A.3

Use the results of Exercise A.1 to multiply 1,000 by 1,000,000 and check that adding their logarithms will give the logarithm of the product.

We might also expect to find that dividing two numbers is equivalent to *subtracting* their logarithms, and this is so:

$$\log 1,000 = 3$$
$$\log 100 = 2$$
$$\log (1,000 \div 100) = 1 = \log 10.$$

Exercise A.4

Divide 10,000 by 10 using logarithms.

Now let us try to divide a smaller number by a larger one and see what happens.

$$\text{Take } 100 \div 10,000 = 0 \cdot 01.$$
$$\log 100 = 2$$
$$\log 10,000 = 4$$
$$\text{Difference} \qquad -\bar{2}$$

If our subtraction rule still holds, -2 must be the logarithm of $0 \cdot 01$. Negative logarithms are used in this way to represent numbers less than 1.

Exercise A.5

Find the logarithm of $0 \cdot 1$ by dividing 10 by 100.

If the answer to part (*c*) of Exercise A.2 has been worrying you, this dividing rule may help. Any number (except zero) divided by itself must give the answer 1, and the difference of the logarithms will be zero. With the introduction of negative logarithms, the original idea of multiplying ten by itself a certain number of times flies out of the window. This is just as well, because we can go on now to consider *fractional* logarithms which will allow us to deal with *any* number and not merely multiples of ten. To summarize: Any positive arithmetical number has a corresponding logarithm. Adding the logarithms of two numbers will give the logarithm of their product.

We sometimes speak of **transforming** a number into its logarithm, and transforming the logarithm back into the original number or **antilogarithm**.

Exercise A.6

Transform 10 into its antilogarithm.

Now look at the following multiplication:

$$3 \cdot 162 \times 3 \cdot 162 = 10.$$

We do not yet know the logarithm of $3 \cdot 162$, but we do know from our addition rule that log $3 \cdot 162 +$ log $3 \cdot 162 = 1$, because 1 is log 10. The logarithm of $3 \cdot 162$ must, therefore, be one-half, or $0 \cdot 5$. Just as $3 \cdot 162$ (the square root of 10) may be calculated by an arithmetical method (which most of us have forgotten), so we can calculate that $1 \cdot 778$ is the square root of $3 \cdot 162$. Its logarithm is, therefore, $0 \cdot 5 \times 0 \cdot 5 = 0 \cdot 25$.

Exercise A.7

The cube root of 10 is $2 \cdot 154$, so

$$2 \cdot 154 \times 2 \cdot 154 \times 2 \cdot 154 = 10.$$

What is log $2 \cdot 154$, to three decimal places?

Exercise A.8

(*a*) $3 \cdot 162 \times 2 \cdot 154 = 6 \cdot 813$.
    What is log $6 \cdot 813$?
(*b*) $3 \cdot 162 \div 2 \cdot 154 = 1 \cdot 467$.
    What is log $1 \cdot 467$?

By using a good deal of ingenuity and ploughing through the tedious arithmetic, we could build up a set of logarithms which should help us to multiply *any* two numbers together, even if they involved fractions. Professional compilers have done just this, producing tables of logarithms for the rest of us to use. Here is a simple example of one.

The numbers in this table increase by uniform steps, but their logarithms do not, as the last column of Table A.I shows.

TABLE A.I

Logarithms of whole numbers from 1 to 10

Number	Logarithm	Differences
1	0	—
2	0·301	0·301
3	0·477	0·176
4	0·602	0·125
5	0·699	0·097
6	0·778	0·079
7	0·845	0·067
8	0·903	0·058
9	0·954	0·051
10	1·000	0·046

Exercise A.9

How may the differences in the last column be interpreted, and does this help to explain why they get smaller as the numbers increase?

Exercise A.10

(*a*) What is the approximate antilogarithm of 0·9?
(*b*) Calculate log 15.
(*c*) 'The average of log 8 and log 2 is log 4'.
Is this true? If so, why?

(*d*) Calculate log 3·5.
(*e*) Calculate log 0·5.
(*f*) Calculate log 0·03.

We have already seen that fractional numbers have negative logarithms, and this is shown in the last examples in Exercise A.10. Let us now compile a table of logarithms for fractional numbers.

The logarithms in the middle column of Table A.II were obtained by subtracting the entries in Table A.I from 1 and consequently the two tables look different. It is inconvenient to have different tables for whole

TABLE A.II

Logarithms of Fractions from 0·1 to 1

Number	Logarithm	Complementary Form
0·1	− 1·000	$\bar{1}$·000
0·2	− 0·699	$\bar{1}$·301
0·3	− 0·523	$\bar{1}$·477
0·4	− 0·398	$\bar{1}$·602
0·5	− 0·301	$\bar{1}$·699
0·6	− 0·222	$\bar{1}$·778
0·7	− 0·155	$\bar{1}$·845
0·8	− 0·097	$\bar{1}$·903
0·9	− 0·046	$\bar{1}$·954
1·0	0	

numbers and fractions, so the device used in the last column of Table A.II is adopted. The entry for, say, 0·4 is $\bar{1}$·602 (read as 'bar-one point six zero two'). This means that the logarithm is made up of a negative part and a positive part. The negative part is always the whole number to the left of the decimal point, and we put the minus sign above it; the positive part is the fraction to the right of the decimal point. In this way we are enabled to derive the logarithms of fractions easily from the table for whole numbers.

Exercise A.11

What is the antilogarithm of
(a) $\bar{1}$·845?
(b) $\bar{2}$·000?
(c) $\bar{2}$·845?

If you think this over for a while, you will see that the fractional part of a logarithm, called its **mantissa**, depends on the string of digits which make up the number, whereas the whole number part, called the **characteristic**, tells us where to put the decimal point and how many zeros to add if necessary. So, since

$$\log 3·162 = 0·5,$$

we have

log 0·3162 = $\bar{1}$·5	log 31·62 = 1·5
log 0·03162 = $\bar{2}$·5	log 316·2 = 2·5
log 0·003162 = $\bar{3}$·5	log 3162 = 3·5
	log 31620 = 4·5

Exercise A.12

(*a*) What is the characteristic of:
log 316·2?   log 785?   log 21,972?
  (*b*) What is the mantissa of log 9?   of log 90?
  (*c*) Multiply 0·3162 by 31·62 using logarithms.

This is as much as you need to know about the theory of logarithms at this stage. All that remains is to learn how to use log tables. The first point to note is that the tables give only the mantissa: you have to work out the characteristic for yourself. Decimal points are also omitted.

By extending Table A.I into greater detail, we get Table A.III.

TABLE A.III

Part of more Detailed Table of Logarithms

Number	Logarithm
1·0	·0000
1·1	·0414
1·2	·0792
1·3	·1139
1·4	·1461
1·5	·1761
etc. to	
9·8	·9912
9·9	·9956

Exercise A.13

Table A.III tells us that the mantissa of log 1·1 is '·0414'.
(*a*) What is the characteristic of log 11?
(*b*) What is log 11?
(*c*) What is log 98?
(*d*) What is log 150?
(*e*) What is log 0·13?
(*f*) What is log 0·00011?
(*g*) Multiply 0·00011 by a million, using logarithms.

Exercise A.14

Suppose that Table A.III had only given us the logarithms of *even* numbers. Estimate approximate values for log 13 and log 99.

Exercise A.15

In the previous exercise you obtained an approximate value for log 13. This approximation is the *exact* logarithm of some number near to 13. Without actually calculating it, say how you could find out what this number is.

Finding intermediate values as in Exercise A.14 is known as *linear interpolation*. It is obviously not very reliable when the difference between successive logarithms is large, but gives good estimates for small differences.

Table A.IV is an extension of Table A.III which gives a more detailed range of values. Its first two columns are simply a repetition of Table A.III, the heading '·00' showing that the third and fourth digits are zero. Similarly the heading '·01' means that 0·0043 is log 1·01, 0·0453 is log 1·11 and so on. Similarly, 0·0086 is log 1·02, 0·0128 is log 1·03.

Exercise A.16

(*a*) What is log 1·54? log 154?
(*b*) What is log 2·16? log 0·216?
(*c*) What is log 2·165?

Exercise A.17

(*a*) What number has 0·2122 as its logarithm?
(*b*) What is the antilogarithm of 0·2122?
(*c*) What is the antilogarithm of 3·2122?
(*d*) Estimate antilog 0·3021.

Exercise A.17 shows that a table of logarithms may be used backwards as a means of finding antilogarithms, but tables of antilogarithms may be used instead: they will be described later. Before doing so, we shall take the final step necessary for a complete understanding of conventional tables of logarithms, such as Table A.V. This is the full version of Table A.IV, but with some extra entries in the columns for ·001, ·002, etc. Let us return for a moment to the working of Exercise A.16 (*c*):

$$\left. \begin{array}{l} \log 2·16 = 0·3345 \\ \log 2·17 = 0·3365 \end{array} \right\} \text{Difference} = 0·0020$$

TABLE A.IV

Part of Detailed Table of Logarithms, extended into Columns

	·00	·01	·02	·03	·04	·05	·06	·07	·08	·09
1·0	·0000	·0043	·0086	·0128	·0170					
						·0212	·0253	·0294	·0334	·0374
1·1	·0414	·0453	·0492	·0531	·0569					
						·0607	·0645	·0682	·0719	·0755
1·2	·0792	·0828	·0864	·0899	·0934					
						·0969	·1004	·1038	·1072	·1106
1·3	·1139	·1173	·1206	·1239	·1271					
						·1303	·1335	·1367	·1399	·1430
1·4	·1461	·1492	·1523	·1553	·1584					
						·1614	·1644	·1673	·1703	·1732
1·5	·1761	·1790	·1818	·1847	·1875					
						·1903	·1931	·1959	·1987	·2014
1·6	·2041	·2068	·2095	·2122	·2148					
						·2175	·2201	·2227	·2253	·2279
1·7	·2304	·2330	·2355	·2380	·2405					
						·2430	·2455	·2480	·2504	·2529
1·8	·2553	·2577	·2601	·2625	·2648					
						·2672	·2695	·2718	·2742	·2765
1·9	·2788	·2810	·2833	·2856	·2878					
						·2900	·2923	·2945	·2967	·2989
2·0	·3010	·3032	·3054	·3075	·3096	·3118	·3139	·3160	·3181	·3201
2·1	·3222	·3243	·3263	·3284	·3304	·3324	·3345	·3365	·3385	·3404
2·2	·3424	·3444	·3464	·3483,	·3502	·3522	·3541	·3560	·3579	·3598
2·3	·3617	·3636	·3655	·3674	·3692	·3711	·3729	·3747	·3766	·3784
2·4	·3802	·3820	·3838	·3856	·3874	·3892	·3909	·3927	·3945	·3962

The difference in the logarithms, 0·0020, corresponds to a difference of 0·01 in the *numbers*, so a difference of 0·001 in the numbers would be matched by a difference of 0·0002 in the logarithms; by this linear interpolation we can deduce that:

$$\log 2 \cdot 161 = 0 \cdot 3345 + 0 \cdot 0002 = 0 \cdot 3347$$
$$\log 2 \cdot 162 = 0 \cdot 3345 + 0 \cdot 0004 = 0 \cdot 3349$$
$$\log 2 \cdot 163 = 0 \cdot 3345 + 0 \cdot 0006 = 0 \cdot 3351$$
$$\log 2 \cdot 164 = 0 \cdot 3345 + 0 \cdot 0008 = 0 \cdot 3353$$
$$\log 2 \cdot 165 = 0 \cdot 3345 + 0 \cdot 0010 = 0 \cdot 3355$$
etc.

The small interpolations, shorn of their initial zeros, are the entries in the last nine columns along the row labelled 2·1: this row contains the logarithms—the mantissae, that is—of 2·16 and 2·17. So to find $\log 2 \cdot 165$ we have only to find $\log 2 \cdot 16$ (·3345), look up the fourth digit (·005) in the differences and find its entry (10), add this to ·3345 to give ·3355 and put the characteristic (0) in front of the decimal point.

Here is the process for $\log 31 \cdot 62$:

1. Enter tables at row 3·1
   Look under column ·06   ·4997
2. Enter last nine columns
   Look under column ·002   3
3. Add these   ·5000
4. Calculate characteristic   1
5. Add to mantissa   1·5000

Exercise A.18

Find the logarithms of:

(a) 2·154
(b) 1·065
(c) 0·00001
(d) 0·00001065
(e) 2,154,000

The figures in these last nine columns are the *mean* differences between successive figures in a row; they may differ slightly at the end of a row, but using the mean value gives only very small rounding errors.

The use of the mean differences columns has been explained here for the sake of completeness, since by convention they are included in most sets of log tables. To many (including myself) they are superfluous, since the difference is easily obtained by subtracting successive entries in the main table.

Any sales manager who is inclined to worry about accuracy in the fourth digit should consider very carefully whether the number itself is known with such great precision, and how great the fourth-figure error will be in comparison with the forecasting error.

Tables of Antilogarithms

The table of antilogarithms is set out in Table A.VI. It is used in much the same way as a log table. For instance, to find antilog 0·1875:

Enter the table at row ·18, column 7   1538
Look up the mean difference in
column 5   2
Add   1540

What about the decimal point? Since the characteristic of the logarithm 0·1875 was 0, its antilog must lie between 1 and 10, so the number must be 1·54.

Exercise A.19

Find antilog 2·1875.

So in looking up antilogs we must first subtract the characteristic and use it to decide the range of values within which the antilog will lie. Then we enter the tables with the mantissa. The absence of the decimal point in the antilog tables serves to distinguish them from ordinary log tables.

The exercise which follows will provide the practice which is essential to the fluent use of logarithms.

Exercise A.20

(a) 3·142 × 2·786
(b) 7·65 ÷ 3·51
(c) 4·189 × 60·33
(d) 0·5122 × 148·7
(e) 0·512247 × 60·33

(f) $0 \cdot 51224 \div 60 \cdot 33$
(g) $84 \cdot 92 \times 1 \cdot 065 \times 1 \cdot 065$
(h) $(1 \cdot 065)^2$
(k) $(1 \cdot 065)^3$
(l) $250,000 \times (1 \cdot 065)^3$

Exercise A.21

The company's economists expect the market to increase at the rate of 6·5 per cent a year for the next few years and the Marketing Manager expects to hold the market share steady. If we sold 250,000 items in 1968, how many do we expect to sell in 1971?

TABLE A.V

LOGARITHMS

	·00	·01	·02	·03	·04	·05	·06	·07	·08	·09	·001	·002	·003	·004	·005	·006	·007	·008	·009
1·0	·0000	·0043	·0086	·0128	·0170						5	9	13	17	21	26	30	34	38
						·0212	·0253	·0294	·0334	·0374	4	8	12	16	20	24	28	32	36
1·1	·0414	·0453	·0492	·0531	·0569						4	8	12	16	20	23	27	31	35
						·0607	·0645	·0682	·0719	·0755	4	7	11	15	18	22	26	29	33
1·2	·0792	·0828	·0864	·0899	·0934						3	7	11	14	18	21	25	28	32
						·0969	·1004	·1038	·1072	·1106	3	7	10	14	17	20	24	27	31
1·3	·1139	·1173	·1206	·1239	·1271						3	6	10	13	16	19	23	26	29
						·1303	·1335	·1367	·1399	·1430	3	7	10	13	16	19	22	25	29
1·4	·1461	·1492	·1523	·1553	·1584						3	6	9	12	15	19	22	25	28
						·1614	·1644	·1673	·1703	·1732	3	6	9	12	14	17	20	23	26
1·5	·1761	·1790	·1818	·1847	·1875						3	6	9	11	14	17	20	23	26
						·1903	·1931	·1959	·1987	·2014	3	6	8	11	14	17	19	22	25
1·6	·2041	·2068	·2095	·2122	·2148						3	6	8	11	14	16	19	22	24
						·2175	·2201	·2227	·2253	·2279	3	5	8	10	13	16	18	21	23
1·7	·2304	·2330	·2355	·2380	·2405						3	5	8	10	13	15	18	20	23
						·2430	·2455	·2480	·2504	·2529	3	5	8	10	12	15	17	20	22
1·8	·2553	·2577	·2601	·2625	·2648						2	5	7	9	12	14	17	19	21
						·2672	·2695	·2718	·2742	·2765	2	4	7	9	11	14	16	18	21
1·9	·2788	·2810	·2833	·2856	·2878						2	4	7	9	11	13	16	18	20
						·2900	·2923	·2945	·2967	·2989	2	4	6	8	11	13	15	17	19
2·0	·3010	·3032	·3054	·3075	·3096	·3118	·3139	·3160	·3181	·3201	2	4	6	8	11	13	15	17	19
2·1	·3222	·3243	·3263	·3284	·3304	·3324	·3345	·3365	·3385	·3404	2	4	6	8	10	12	14	16	18
2·2	·3424	·3444	·3464	·3483	·3502	·3522	·3541	·3560	·3579	·3598	2	4	6	8	10	12	14	15	17
2·3	·3617	·3636	·3655	·3674	·3692	·3711	·3729	·3747	·3766	·3784	2	4	6	7	9	11	13	15	17
2·4	·3802	·3820	·3838	·3856	·3874	·3892	·3909	·3927	·3945	·3962	2	4	5	7	9	11	12	14	16
2·5	·3979	·3997	·4014	·4031	·4048	·4065	·4082	·4099	·4116	·4133	2	3	5	7	9	10	12	14	15
2·6	·4150	·4166	·4183	·4200	·4216	·4232	·4249	·4265	·4281	·4298	2	3	5	7	8	10	11	13	15
2·7	·4314	·4330	·4346	·4362	·4378	·4393	·4409	·4425	·4440	·4456	2	3	5	6	8	9	11	13	14
2·8	·4472	·4487	·4502	·4518	·4533	·4548	·4564	·4579	·4594	·4609	2	3	5	6	8	9	11	12	14
2·9	·4624	·4639	·4654	·4669	·4683	·4698	·4713	·4728	·4742	·4757	1	3	4	6	7	9	10	12	13
3·0	·4771	·4786	·4800	·4814	·4829	·4843	·4857	·4871	·4886	·4900	1	3	4	6	7	9	10	11	13
3·1	·4914	·4928	·4942	·4955	·4969	·4983	·4997	·5011	·5024	·5038	1	3	4	6	7	8	10	11	12
3·2	·5051	·5065	·5079	·5092	·5105	·5119	·5132	·5145	·5159	·5172	1	3	4	5	7	8	9	11	12
3·3	·5185	·5198	·5211	·5224	·5237	·5250	·5263	·5276	·5289	·5302	1	3	4	5	6	8	9	10	12
3·4	·5315	·5328	·5340	·5353	·5366	·5378	·5391	·5403	·5416	·5428	1	3	4	5	6	8	9	10	11
3·5	·5441	·5453	·5465	·5478	·5490	·5502	·5514	·5527	·5539	·5551	1	2	4	5	6	7	9	10	11
3·6	·5563	·5575	·5587	·5599	·5611	·5623	·5635	·5647	·5658	·5670	1	2	4	5	6	7	8	10	11
3·7	·5682	·5694	·5705	·5717	·5729	·5740	·5752	·5763	·5775	·5786	1	2	3	5	6	7	8	9	10
3·8	·5798	·5809	·5821	·5832	·5843	·5855	·5866	·5877	·5888	·5899	1	2	3	5	6	7	8	9	10
3·9	·5911	·5922	·5933	·5944	·5955	·5966	·5977	·5988	·5999	·6010	1	2	3	4	5	7	8	9	10
4·0	·6021	·6031	·6042	·6053	·6064	·6075	·6085	·6096	·6107	·6117	1	2	3	4	5	6	8	9	10
4·1	·6128	·6138	·6149	·6160	·6170	·6180	·6191	·6201	·6212	·6222	1	2	3	4	5	6	7	8	9
4·2	·6232	·6243	·6253	·6263	·6274	·6284	·6294	·6304	·6314	·6325	1	2	3	4	5	6	7	8	9
4·3	·6335	·6345	·6355	·6365	·6375	·6385	·6395	·6405	·6415	·6425	1	2	3	4	5	6	7	8	9
4·4	·6435	·6444	·6454	·6464	·6474	·6484	·6493	·6503	·6513	·6522	1	2	3	4	5	6	7	8	9
4·5	·6532	·6542	·6551	·6561	·6571	·6580	·6590	·6599	·6609	·6618	1	2	3	4	5	6	7	8	9
4·6	·6628	·6637	·6646	·6656	·6665	·6675	·6684	·6693	·6702	·6712	1	2	3	4	5	6	7	7	8
4·7	·6721	·6730	·6739	·6749	·6758	·6767	·6776	·6785	·6794	·6803	1	2	3	4	5	5	6	7	8
4·8	·6812	·6821	·6830	·6839	·6848	·6857	·6866	·6875	·6884	·6893	1	2	3	4	4	5	6	7	8
4·9	·6902	·6911	·6920	·6928	·6937	·6946	·6955	·6964	·6972	·6981	1	2	3	4	4	5	6	7	8

10,000ths

LOGARITHMS

	0·0	·01	·02	·03	·04	·05	·06	·07	·08	·09	·001	·002	·003	·004	·005	·006	·007	·008	·009
5·0	·6990	·6998	·7007	·7016	·7024	·7033	·7042	·7050	·7059	·7067	1	2	3	3	4	5	6	7	8
5·1	·7076	·7084	·7093	·7101	·7110	·7118	·7126	·7135	·7143	·7152	1	2	3	3	4	5	6	7	8
5·2	·7160	·7168	·7177	·7185	·7193	·7202	·7210	·7218	·7226	·7235	1	2	2	3	4	5	6	7	7
5·3	·7243	·7251	·7259	·7267	·7275	·7284	·7292	·7300	·7308	·7316	1	2	2	3	4	5	6	6	7
5·4	·7324	·7332	·7340	·7348	·7356	·7364	·7372	·7380	·7388	·7396	1	2	2	3	4	5	6	6	7
5·5	·7404	·7412	·7419	·7427	·7435	·7443	·7451	·7459	·7466	·7474	1	2	2	3	4	5	5	6	7
5·6	·7482	·7490	·7497	·7505	·7513	·7520	·7528	·7536	·7543	·7551	1	2	2	3	4	5	5	6	7
5·7	·7559	·7566	·7574	·7582	·7589	·7597	·7604	·7612	·7619	·7627	1	2	2	3	4	5	5	6	7
5·8	·7634	·7642	·7649	·7657	·7664	·7672	·7679	·7686	·7694	·7701	1	1	2	3	4	4	5	6	7
5·9	·7709	·7716	·7723	·7731	·7738	·7745	·7752	·7760	·7767	·7774	1	1	2	3	4	4	5	6	7
6·0	·7782	·7789	·7796	·7803	·7810	·7818	·7825	·7832	·7839	·7846	1	1	2	3	4	4	5	6	6
6·1	·7853	·7860	·7868	·7875	·7882	·7889	·7896	·7903	·7910	·7917	1	1	2	3	4	4	5	6	6
6·2	·7924	·7931	·7938	·7945	·7952	·7959	·7966	·7973	·7980	·7987	1	1	2	3	3	4	5	6	6
6·3	·7993	·8000	·8007	·8014	·8021	·8028	·8035	·8041	·8048	·8055	1	1	2	3	3	4	5	5	6
6·4	·8062	·8069	·8075	·8082	·8089	·8096	·8102	·8109	·8116	·8122	1	1	2	3	3	4	5	5	6
6·5	·8129	·8136	·8142	·8149	·8156	·8162	·8169	·8176	·8182	·8189	1	1	2	3	3	4	5	5	6
6·6	·8195	·8202	·8209	·8215	·8222	·8228	·8235	·8241	·8248	·8254	1	1	2	3	3	4	5	5	6
6·7	·8261	·8267	·8274	·8280	·8287	·8293	·8299	·8306	·8312	·8319	1	1	2	3	3	4	5	5	6
6·8	·8325	·8331	·8338	·8344	·8351	·8357	·8363	·8370	·8376	·8382	1	1	2	3	3	4	4	5	6
6·9	·8388	·8395	·8401	·8407	·8414	·8420	·8426	·8432	·8439	·8445	1	1	2	2	3	4	4	5	6
7·0	·8451	·8457	·8463	·8470	·8476	·8482	·8488	·8494	·8500	·8506	1	1	2	2	3	4	4	5	6
7·1	·8513	·8519	·8525	·8531	·8537	·8543	·8549	·8555	·8561	·8567	1	1	2	2	3	4	4	5	5
7·2	·8573	·8579	·8585	·8591	·8597	·8603	·8609	·8615	·8621	·8627	1	1	2	2	3	4	4	5	5
7·3	·8633	·8639	·8645	·8651	·8657	·8663	·8669	·8675	·8681	·8686	1	1	2	2	3	4	4	5	5
7·4	·8692	·8698	·8704	·8710	·8716	·8722	·8727	·8733	·8739	·8745	1	1	2	2	3	4	4	5	5
7·5	·8751	·8756	·8762	·8768	·8774	·8779	·8785	·8791	·8797	·8802	1	1	2	2	3	3	4	5	5
7·6	·8808	·8814	·8820	·8825	·8831	·8837	·8842	·8848	·8854	·8859	1	1	2	2	3	3	4	5	5
7·7	·8865	·8871	·8876	·8882	·8887	·8893	·8899	·8904	·8910	·8915	1	1	2	2	3	3	4	4	5
7·8	·8921	·8927	·8932	·8938	·8943	·8949	·8954	·8960	·8965	·8971	1	1	2	2	3	3	4	4	5
7·9	·8976	·8982	·8987	·8993	·8998	·9004	·9009	·9015	·9020	·9025	1	1	2	2	3	3	4	4	5
8·0	·9031	·9036	·9042	·9047	·9053	·9058	·9063	·9069	·9074	·9079	1	1	2	2	3	3	4	4	5
8·1	·9085	·9090	·9096	·9101	·9106	·9112	·9117	·9122	·9128	·9133	1	1	2	2	3	3	4	4	5
8·2	·9138	·9143	·9149	·9154	·9159	·9165	·9170	·9175	·9180	·9186	1	1	2	2	3	3	4	4	5
8·3	·9191	·9196	·9201	·9206	·9212	·9217	·9222	·9227	·9232	·9238	1	1	2	2	3	3	4	4	5
8·4	·9243	·9248	·9253	·9258	·9263	·9269	·9274	·9279	·9284	·9289	1	1	2	2	3	3	4	4	5
8·5	·9294	·9299	·9304	·9309	·9315	·9320	·9325	·9330	·9335	·9340	1	1	2	2	3	3	4	4	5
8·6	·9345	·9350	·9355	·9360	·9365	·9370	·9375	·9380	·9385	·9390	1	1	2	2	3	3	4	4	5
8·7	·9395	·9400	·9405	·9410	·9415	·9420	·9425	·9430	·9435	·9440	0	1	1	2	2	3	3	4	4
8·8	·9445	·9450	·9455	·9460	·9465	·9469	·9474	·9479	·9484	·9489	0	1	1	2	2	3	3	4	4
8·9	·9494	·9499	·9504	·9509	·9513	·9518	·9523	·9528	·9533	·9538	0	1	1	2	2	3	3	4	4
9·0	·9542	·9547	·9552	·9557	·9562	·9566	·9571	·9576	·9581	·9586	0	1	1	2	2	3	3	4	4
9·1	·9590	·9595	·9600	·9605	·9609	·9614	·9619	·9624	·9628	·9633	0	1	1	2	2	3	3	4	4
9·2	·9638	·9643	·9647	·9652	·9657	·9661	·9666	·9671	·9675	·9680	0	1	1	2	2	3	3	4	4
9·3	·9685	·9689	·9694	·9699	·9703	·9708	·9713	·9717	·9722	·9727	0	1	1	2	2	3	3	4	4
9·4	·9731	·9736	·9741	·9745	·9750	·9754	·9759	·9763	·9768	·9773	0	1	1	2	2	3	3	4	4
9·5	·9777	·9782	·9786	·9791	·9795	·9800	·9805	·9809	·9814	·9818	0	1	1	2	2	3	3	4	4
9·6	·9823	·9827	·9832	·9836	·9841	·9845	·9850	·9854	·9859	·9863	0	1	1	2	2	3	3	4	4
9·7	·9868	·9872	·9877	·9881	·9886	·9890	·9894	·9899	·9903	·9908	0	1	1	2	2	3	3	4	4
9·8	·9912	·9917	·9921	·9926	·9930	·9934	·9939	·9943	·9948	·9952	0	1	1	2	2	3	3	4	4
9·9	·9956	·9961	·9965	·9969	·9974	·9978	·9983	·9987	·9991	·9996	0	1	1	2	2	3	3	3	4

10,000ths

TABLE A.VI

ANTI-LOGARITHMS

	0	1	2	3	4	5	6	7	8	9	1 2 3 4	5	6 7 8 9
·00	1000	1002	1005	1007	1009	1012	1014	1016	1019	1021	0 0 1 1	1	1 2 2 2
·01	1023	1026	1028	1030	1033	1035	1038	1040	1042	1045	0 0 1 1	1	1 2 2 2
·02	1047	1050	1052	1054	1057	1059	1062	1064	1067	1069	0 0 1 1	1	1 2 2 2
·03	1072	1074	1076	1079	1081	1084	1086	1089	1091	1094	0 0 1 1	1	1 2 2 2
·04	1096	1099	1102	1104	1107	1109	1112	1114	1117	1119	0 1 1 1	1	2 2 2 2
·05	1122	1125	1127	1130	1132	1135	1138	1140	1143	1146	0 1 1 1	1	2 2 2 2
·06	1148	1151	1153	1156	1159	1161	1164	1167	1169	1172	0 1 1 1	1	2 2 2 2
·07	1175	1178	1180	1183	1186	1189	1191	1194	1197	1199	0 1 1 1	1	2 2 2 2
·08	1202	1205	1208	1211	1213	1216	1219	1222	1225	1227	0 1 1 1	1	2 2 2 3
·09	1230	1233	1236	1239	1242	1245	1247	1250	1253	1256	0 1 1 1	1	2 2 2 3
·10	1259	1262	1265	1268	1271	1274	1276	1279	1282	1285	0 1 1 1	1	2 2 2 3
·11	1288	1291	1294	1297	1300	1303	1306	1309	1312	1315	0 1 1 1	2	2 2 2 3
·12	1318	1321	1324	1327	1330	1334	1337	1340	1343	1346	0 1 1 1	2	2 2 2 3
·13	1349	1352	1355	1358	1361	1365	1368	1371	1374	1377	0 1 1 1	2	2 2 3 3
·14	1380	1384	1387	1390	1393	1396	1400	1403	1406	1409	0 1 1 1	2	2 2 3 3
·15	1413	1416	1419	1422	1426	1429	1432	1435	1439	1442	0 1 1 1	2	2 2 3 3
·16	1445	1449	1452	1455	1459	1462	1466	1469	1472	1476	0 1 1 1	2	2 2 3 3
·17	1479	1483	1486	1489	1493	1496	1500	1503	1507	1510	0 1 1 1	2	2 2 3 3
·18	1514	1517	1521	1524	1528	1531	1535	1538	1542	1545	0 1 1 1	2	2 2 3 3
·19	1549	1552	1556	1560	1563	1567	1570	1574	1578	1581	0 1 1 1	2	2 3 3 3
·20	1585	1589	1592	1596	1600	1603	1607	1611	1614	1618	0 1 1 1	2	2 3 3 3
·21	1622	1626	1629	1633	1637	1641	1644	1648	1652	1656	0 1 1 2	2	2 3 3 3
·22	1660	1663	1667	1671	1675	1679	1683	1687	1690	1694	0 1 1 2	2	2 3 3 3
·23	1698	1702	1706	1710	1714	1718	1722	1726	1730	1734	0 1 1 2	2	2 3 3 4
·24	1738	1742	1746	1750	1754	1758	1762	1766	1770	1774	0 1 1 2	2	2 3 3 4
·25	1778	1782	1786	1791	1795	1799	1803	1807	1811	1816	0 1 1 2	2	2 3 3 4
·26	1820	1824	1828	1832	1837	1841	1845	1849	1854	1858	0 1 1 2	2	3 3 3 4
·27	1862	1866	1871	1875	1879	1884	1888	1892	1897	1901	0 1 1 2	2	3 3 3 4
·28	1905	1910	1914	1919	1923	1928	1932	1936	1941	1945	0 1 1 2	2	3 3 4 4
·29	1950	1954	1959	1963	1968	1972	1977	1982	1986	1991	0 1 1 2	2	3 3 4 4
·30	1995	2000	2004	2009	2014	2018	2023	2028	2032	2037	0 1 1 2	2	3 3 4 4
·31	2042	2046	2051	2056	2061	2065	2070	2075	2080	2084	0 1 1 2	2	3 3 4 4
·32	2089	2094	2099	2104	2109	2113	2118	2123	2128	2133	0 1 1 2	2	3 3 4 4
·33	2138	2143	2148	2153	2158	2163	2168	2173	2178	2183	0 1 1 2	2	3 3 4 4
·34	2188	2193	2198	2203	2208	2213	2218	2223	2228	2234	1 1 2 2	3	3 4 4 5
·35	2239	2244	2249	2254	2259	2265	2270	2275	2280	2286	1 1 2 2	3	3 4 4 5
·36	2291	2296	2301	2307	2312	2317	2323	2328	2333	2339	1 1 2 2	3	3 4 4 5
·37	2344	2350	2355	2360	2366	2371	2377	2382	2388	2393	1 1 2 2	3	3 4 4 5
·38	2399	2404	2410	2415	2421	2427	2432	2438	2443	2449	1 1 2 2	3	3 4 4 5
·39	2455	2460	2466	2472	2477	2483	2489	2495	2500	2506	1 1 2 2	3	3 4 5 5
·40	2512	2518	2523	2529	2535	2541	2547	2553	2559	2564	1 1 2 2	3	4 4 5 5
·41	2570	2576	2582	2588	2594	2600	2606	2612	2618	2624	1 1 2 2	3	4 4 5 5
·42	2630	2636	2642	2649	2655	2661	2667	2673	2679	2685	1 1 2 2	3	4 4 5 6
·43	2692	2698	2704	2710	2716	2723	2729	2735	2742	2748	1 1 2 3	3	4 4 5 6
·44	2754	2761	2767	2773	2780	2786	2793	2799	2805	2812	1 1 2 3	3	4 4 5 6
·45	2818	2825	2831	2838	2844	2851	2858	2864	2871	2877	1 1 2 3	3	4 5 5 6
·46	2884	2891	2897	2904	2911	2917	2924	2931	2938	2944	1 1 2 3	3	4 5 5 6
·47	2951	2958	2965	2972	2979	2985	2992	2999	3006	3013	1 1 2 3	3	4 5 5 6
·48	3020	3027	3034	3041	3048	3055	3062	3069	3076	3083	1 1 2 3	4	4 5 6 6
·49	3090	3097	3105	3112	3119	3126	3133	3141	3148	3155	1 1 2 3	4	4 5 6 6

ANTI-LOGARITHMS

	0	1	2	3	4	5	6	7	8	9	1 2 3 4	5	6 7 8 9
·50	3162	3170	3177	3184	3192	3199	3206	3214	3221	3228	1 1 2 3	4	4 5 6 7
·51	3236	3243	3251	3258	3266	3273	3281	3289	3296	3304	1 2 2 3	4	5 5 6 7
·52	3311	3319	3327	3334	3342	3350	3357	3365	3373	3381	1 2 2 3	4	5 5 6 7
·53	3388	3396	3404	3412	3420	3428	3436	3443	3451	3459	1 2 2 3	4	5 6 6 7
·54	3467	3475	3483	3491	3499	3508	3516	3524	3532	3540	1 2 2 3	4	5 6 6 7
·55	3548	3556	3565	3573	3581	3589	3597	3606	3614	3622	1 2 2 3	4	5 6 7 7
·56	3631	3639	3648	3656	3664	3673	3681	3690	3698	3707	1 2 3 3	4	5 6 7 8
·57	3715	3724	3733	3741	3750	3758	3767	3776	3784	3793	1 2 3 3	4	5 6 7 8
·58	3802	3811	3819	3828	3837	3846	3855	3864	3873	3882	1 2 3 4	4	5 6 7 8
·59	3890	3899	3908	3917	3926	3936	3945	3954	3963	3972	1 2 3 4	5	5 6 7 8
·60	3981	3990	3999	4009	4018	4027	4036	4046	4055	4064	1 2 3 4	5	6 6 7 8
·61	4074	4083	4093	4102	4111	4121	4130	4140	4150	4159	1 2 3 4	5	6 7 8 9
·62	4169	4178	4188	4198	4207	4217	4227	4236	4246	4256	1 2 3 4	5	6 7 8 9
·63	4266	4276	4285	4295	4305	4315	4325	4335	4345	4355	1 2 3 4	5	6 7 8 9
·64	4365	4375	4385	4395	4406	4416	4426	4436	4446	4457	1 2 3 4	5	6 7 8 9
·65	4467	4477	4487	4498	4508	4519	4529	4539	4550	4560	1 2 3 4	5	6 7 8 9
·66	4571	4581	4592	4603	4613	4624	4634	4645	4656	4667	1 2 3 4	5	6 7 9 10
·67	4677	4688	4699	4710	4721	4732	4742	4753	4764	4775	1 2 3 4	5	7 8 9 10
·68	4786	4797	4808	4819	4831	4842	4853	4864	4875	4887	1 2 3 4	6	7 8 9 10
·69	4898	4909	4920	4932	4943	4955	4966	4977	4989	5000	1 2 3 5	6	7 8 9 10
·70	5012	5023	5035	5047	5058	5070	5082	5093	5105	5117	1 2 4 5	6	7 8 9 10
·71	5129	5140	5152	5164	5176	5188	5200	5212	5224	5236	1 2 4 5	6	7 8 10 11
·72	5248	5260	5272	5284	5297	5309	5321	5333	5346	5358	1 2 4 5	6	7 9 10 11
·73	5370	5383	5395	5408	5420	5433	5445	5458	5470	5483	1 3 4 5	6	8 9 10 11
·74	5495	5508	5521	5534	5546	5559	5572	5585	5598	5610	1 3 4 5	6	8 9 10 12
·75	5623	5636	5649	5662	5675	5689	5702	5715	5728	5741	1 3 4 5	7	8 9 10 12
·76	5754	5768	5781	5794	5808	5821	5834	5848	5861	5875	1 3 4 5	7	8 9 11 12
·77	5888	5902	5916	5929	5943	5957	5970	5984	5998	6012	1 3 4 5	7	8 10 11 12
·78	6026	6039	6053	6067	6081	6095	6109	6124	6138	6152	1 3 4 6	7	8 10 11 13
·79	6166	6180	6194	6209	6223	6237	6252	6266	6281	6295	1 3 4 6	7	9 10 11 13
·80	6310	6324	6339	6353	6368	6383	6397	6412	6427	6442	1 3 4 6	7	9 10 12 13
·81	6457	6471	6486	6501	6516	6531	6546	6561	6577	6592	2 3 5 6	8	9 11 12 14
·82	6607	6622	6637	6653	6668	6683	6699	6714	6730	6745	2 3 5 6	8	9 11 12 14
·83	6761	6776	6792	6808	6823	6839	6855	6871	6887	6902	2 3 5 6	8	9 11 13 14
·84	6918	6934	6950	6966	6982	6998	7015	7033	7047	7063	2 3 5 6	8	10 11 13 15
·85	7079	7096	7112	7129	7145	7161	7178	7194	7211	7228	2 3 5 7	8	10 12 13 15
·86	7244	7261	7278	7295	7311	7328	7345	7362	7379	7396	2 3 5 7	8	10 12 13 15
·87	7413	7430	7447	7464	7482	7499	7516	7534	7551	7568	2 3 5 7	9	10 12 14 16
·88	7586	7603	7621	7638	7656	7674	7691	7709	7727	7745	2 4 5 7	9	11 12 14 16
·89	7762	7780	7798	7816	7834	7852	7870	7889	7907	7925	2 4 5 7	9	11 13 14 16
·90	7943	7962	7980	7998	8017	8035	8054	8072	8091	8110	2 4 6 7	9	11 13 15 17
·91	8128	8147	8166	8185	8204	8222	8241	8260	8279	8299	2 4 6 7	9	11 13 15 17
·92	8318	8337	8356	8375	8395	8414	8433	8453	8472	8492	2 4 6 8	10	12 14 15 17
·93	8511	8531	8551	8570	8590	8610	8630	8650	8670	8690	2 4 6 8	10	12 14 16 18
·94	8710	8730	8750	8770	8790	8810	8831	8851	8872	8892	2 4 6 8	10	12 14 16 18
·95	8913	8933	8954	8974	8995	9016	9036	9057	9078	9099	2 4 6 8	10	12 15 17 19
·96	9120	9141	9162	9183	9204	9226	9247	9268	9290	9311	2 4 6 8	11	13 15 17 19
·97	9333	9354	9376	9397	9419	9441	9462	9484	9506	9528	2 4 7 9	11	13 15 17 20
·98	9550	9572	9594	9616	9638	9661	9683	9705	9727	9750	2 4 7 9	11	13 16 18 20
·99	9772	9795	9817	9840	9863	9886	9908	9931	9954	9977	2 5 7 9	11	14 16 18 20

I

SOLUTIONS TO EXERCISES

Exercise 1.1

(a) Forecast $=\frac{1}{2}(98,600+114,000)=\textbf{106,300}$

(b) Annual increase $=114,000-98,600=15,400$
Forecast $=114,000+15,400=\textbf{129,400}$

(c) Annual ratio $=114,000\div98,600=1\cdot156$
Forecast $+114,000\times1\cdot156=\textbf{132,000}$

Exercise 1.2

The actual figure, 178,000, shows that neither (a), (b) nor (c) is an adequate assumption. Either a rule must be adopted which gives an even greater increase than (c), or a large random effect must be assumed.

Exercise 1.3

Yes. For heating oil in case (a), our knowledge of the weather reinforces the information inherent in the figures themselves, and the evidence for a seasonal trend is much stronger. For ice cream in case (b), the figures show that sales go down in summer, whereas common sense suggests the opposite. We should be more inclined to ascribe the low summer figures to some temporary, non-recurrent disturbance of business conditions or to large random fluctuations rather than to a seasonal trend.

Exercise 2.1

Base level $=250.$

Random Errors

J	+21	J	-142
F	+12	A	-61
M	+3	S	+37
A	-5	O	+89
M	-136	N	+75
J	-85	D	+192

Total $= +429-429=\textbf{0}$

Exercise 2.2

$$\text{February Adjustment} = \frac{381 - 262}{12} = +10$$

$$\text{New MA} = 263 + 10 = \mathbf{273}$$

$$\text{March Adjustment} = \frac{394 - 253}{12} = +12$$

$$\text{New MA} = 273 + 12 = \mathbf{285}$$

Exercise 2.3

$$\text{February Adjustment} = 3{,}151 - 262 + 381 = 3{,}270$$
$$\text{New MAA} = \mathbf{273}$$
$$\text{March Adjustment} = 3{,}270 - 253 + 394 = 3{,}411$$
$$\text{New MAA} = \mathbf{284}$$

The answers are better than those in the previous exercise because they have smaller rouding errors. In achieving this improvement, we are obliged to carry forward the MAT as well as the MAA, and one may doubt whether the greater accuracy justifies the more cumbersome method.

Exercise 2.4

Month	Sales	Sales in same month of preceding year	Moving Annual Total	Moving Annual Average
—	—	—	1,201	100
J	99	101	1,199	100
F	101	103	1,197	100
M	102	101	1,198	100
A	98	102	1,194	100
M	99	98	1,195	100
J	96	102	1,189	99
J	99	101	1,187	99
A	98	102	1,183	99
S	102	99	1,186	99
O	101	97	1,190	99
N	104	98	1,196	100
D		97		
Annual Total:	1,201			

Exercise 2.5

Since we have no way of knowing what the random error will be in December, our best forecast is the current estimate of the base level. This is the MAA and the forecast is therefore **100**.

Exercise 2.6

So far there is no evidence of a secular trend. If it exists at all, it is small compared with the random errors. The best estimate for all future months, in the absence of any further information, is still 100. This gives a total of **1,200** for the whole year.

Exercise 2.7

Lag = **1 period.**

Exercise 2.8

Lag = **5½ months,** i.e. $\frac{1}{2}(12-1)$.

Exercise 2.9

Month	Sales	Sales in same month of previous year	Moving Annual Total	Moving Annual Average
—	—	—	852	71
J	84←	60	876	73
F	86	62	900	75
M	88	64	924	77
A	90	66	948	79
M	92	68	972	81
J	94	70	996	83
J	96	72	1,020	85←
A	98	74	1,044	87
S	100	76	1,068	89
O	102	78	1,092	91
N	104	80	1,116	93
D	106	82	1,140	95

Annual Total: 1,140   852

Note lag of 5½ months as shown by arrows.

Exercise 2.10

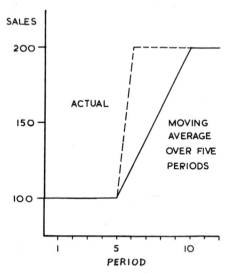

Figure S2.1 Solution to Exercise 2.10

Exercise 2.11

The 3-year moving average would be **more accurate** but **less precise**.

Exercise 2.12

Sum of squares of errors $= 104$
Variance $= 104 \div 22$ $= 4.73$
Standard Deviation $= \mathbf{2 \cdot 2}$

Exercise 2.13

(*a*)   Standard Deviation $= 2 \cdot 2$
    Confidence Limits $= 100 \pm 2 \times 2 \cdot 2$
    $= \mathbf{95 \cdot 6 \text{ to } 104 \cdot 4}$

(*b*) It is well outside the confidence limits, so it seems likely that an upward trend has appeared.

Exercise 2.14

TABLE 2.IV (*continued*)

Year	Thousands of mega-watt hours	3 year MT	3 year MA	Trend	Forecast =3 year MA + 2 × Trend	Error, Forecast − Actual
1961			9·191		10·711	
1962	11·068	30·396	10·132	+0·941	**12·014**	−0·357

Exercise 2.15

The errors are −0·680, −0·107 and −0·357. In other words, the forecasts appear to be consistently low (biassed downwards) and some steeper form of trend might be assumed—multiplicative, for example. However, the evidence afforded by three figures is very slight—the effects could be random.

Exercise 2.16

Month	Sales	Sales in same month of previous year	Moving Annual Total	Moving Annual Average	Trend	Trend Correc-tion	Forecast for next Month
			2053	171			
J	183	161	2075	173	+2	+13	186 (F)
F	187	165	2097	175	+2	+13	188 (M)
M	190	165	2122	177	+2	+13	190 (A)
A	188	168	2142	178	+1	+6	184 (M)
M	191	166	2167	181	+3	+20	201 (J)
J	190	172	2185	182	+1	+6	188 (J)
J	195	173	2207	184	+2	+13	197 (A)
A	196	176	2227	186	+2	+13	199 (S)
S	202	175	2254	188	+2	+13	201 (O)
O	203	175	2282	190	+2	+13	203 (N)
N	208	178	2312	193	+3	+20	213 (D)
D	203	179	2336	195	+2	+13	208 (J)

Annual Total 2053

Note the considerable effects of rounding-off the trend and working from moving averages, and how these are aggravated by multiplying to obtain the trend correction. In April, for instance, the trend obtained from the MATs would be $+1·7$, giving a correction of $+1·7 \times 6·5 = +11$.

Exercise 2.17

$$
\begin{array}{ll}
F & -1 \\
M & -2 \\
A & +2 \\
M & -7 \\
J & +11 \\
J & -6 \\
A & +1 \\
S & -3 \\
O & -2 \\
N & -5 \\
D & +10 \\
\end{array}
$$

(*a*) The total of all these errors is -2; their average is so small that no convincing evidence of bias can be said to exist.

(*b*) The sum of the squares of the errors is 354. Dividing by 10 gives a variance of **35·4**. The square root of this is the standard error, **5·95**, so the confidence limits are about ± 12. These are all measures of the precision of the forecast.

Exercise 2.18

The MAT remains steady at **1 million**, regardless of the month in which it is measured.

Exercise 3·1

Period 1, **0**;   period 2, $\frac{1}{4}$.

Exercise 3·2

(*a*)
$$
\begin{array}{l}
0\cdot1 \times 62 = 6\cdot2 \\
0\cdot2 \times 57 = 11\cdot4 \\
0\cdot3 \times 71 = 21\cdot3 \\
0\cdot4 \times 82 = 32\cdot8 \\
\hline
\end{array}
$$

Weighted moving average = **71·7**

(*b*) **Yes.** The rectangularly-weighted moving average is 68·0, which is less. The triangular weighting gives low weights of 0·1 and 0·2 to the periods of low sales and higher weights to the periods of high sales. Hence the triangular moving average is the higher.

Exercise 3·3

The total in each case is **100**, the weights being given as percentages. In effect, the total is, therefore, 1.

Exercise 3.4

0·02 and **0·01**.

Exercise 3.5

$$0.5 \times \text{New Sales Figure} = 0.5 \times 61.0 = 30.5$$
$$0.5 \times \text{Old EWMA} \quad = 0.5 \times 69.1 = 34.6$$

$$\text{New EWMA} = \mathbf{65.1}$$

Exercise 3.6

(*a*) Yes, **0·8** ($0.200 \times 0.8 = 0.160$, etc.).
(*b*)   Period − 8   **0·042**
                             − 9   **0·034**
                            − 10   **0·027**
(*c*) The total is **0·893**; as more periods are considered, the total approaches 1 more closely.
(*d*) See Figure S3.1 (*overleaf*).

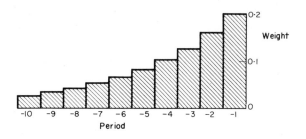

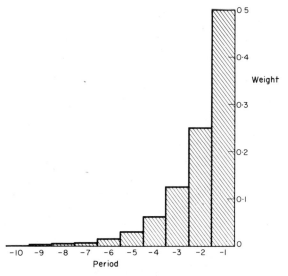

Figure S3.1 Solution to Exercise 3.6 (*d*)

Exercise 3.7

$$1 + 10\% = 1{\cdot}1$$
$$\text{Common ratio} = b = \frac{1}{1{\cdot}1} = 0{\cdot}909$$
$$\therefore \quad a = 1 - 0{\cdot}909 = \mathbf{0{\cdot}091}$$

Exercise 3.8

Period	Sales	EWMA (100)
1	100	**100**
2	100	**100**
3	100	**100**
4	100	**100**
5	100	**100**
6	110	**103**
7	120	**109**
8	130	**116**
9	140	**124**
10	150	**133**
11	160	**142**
12	170	**151**
13	180	**161**
14	190	**171**
15	200	**181**
16	200	**187**
17	200	**191**
18	200	**194**
19	200	**196**
20	200	**197**

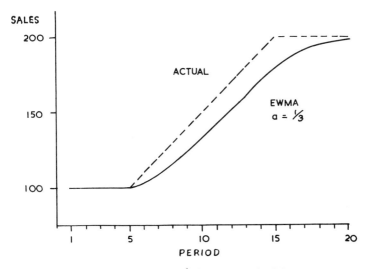

Figure S3.2 Solution to Exercise 3.8

Note the time-lag which in period 15 is approximately equivalent to two periods.

Exercise 3.9

Period	Sales	MA (n=4)	EWMA (a=0·4)
0			75
1	78	—	76·2
2	62	—	70·5
3	57	—	65·1
4	71	67·0	67·5
5	82	68·0	73·3
6	64	68·5	69·6
7	61	69·5	66·2
8	81	72·0	72·1
9	92	74·5	70·1
10	69	75·8	69·7
11	63	76·2	67·0
12	85	77·2	74·2

The graphs are shown in Figure S3.3.

Exercise 3.10

$$n=12, \ a=\frac{2}{12+1}=0·15$$
$$b=1-a \ =\mathbf{0·85}$$

Exercise 3.11

Month	Sales	Forecast (EWMA)	Error (Forecast − Actual)
		50	
J	101	67	−51
F	103	79	−36
M	101	86	−22
A	102	91	−16
M	98	93	−7
J	102	96	−9
J	101	98	−5
A	102	99	−4
S	99	99	0
O	97	98	+2
N	98	98	0
D	97	98	−1

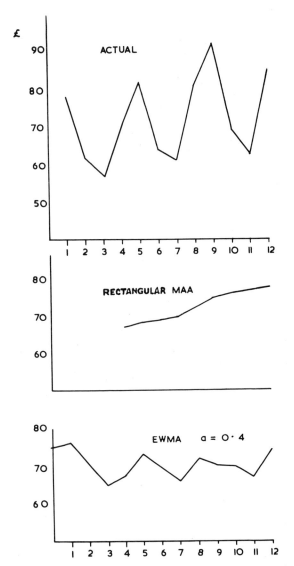

Figure S3.3 Solution to Exercise 3.9. Effect of seasonal trends on EWMA

It is most unlikely that an example such as this would occur in practice. The marketing manager would almost certainly adjust the forecast by March at the latest. Nevertheless, it does show that if by some oversight the automatic forecasting system were left to itself, it would bring the forecast sales up to a reasonably accurate level within a few months, because of its low damping.

Exercise 3.12

Period	Sales	EWMA	Difference between successive EWMAs = Trend	Difference between successive sales
15	200	180·7		
16	210	190·4	+9·7	+10
17	220	200·3	+9·9	+10
18	230	210·2	+9·9	+10
19	240	220·1	+9·9	+10
20	250	230·1	+10·0	+10

Exercise 4.1

		Value Thousands of Mwh	Weight	Value × Weight
Year 1956 = Period 1		6·826	−2·5	−17·065
1957	2	7·125	−1·5	−10·688
1958	3	7·724	−0·5	−3·862
1959	4	8·245	+0·5	+4·122
1960	5	9·324	+1·5	+13·986
1961	6	10·004	+2·5	+25·010
Average: 3·5		8·208	Total	+11·503 = Numerator

Sum of squares of weights: 17·5 = Denominator

$$\text{Linear Regression Coefficient} = +\frac{11·503}{17·5} = +0·657$$

i.e. **Demand is increasing by 0·657 Mwh a year.**

Exercise 4.2

Forecast for 1962 = 8·208 + 3·5 × 0·657 = **10·508.**
(The actual value was 11·068.)
Forecast for 1963 = 8·208 + 4·5 × 0·657 = **11·164.**
(A quicker method for 1963 would be 10·508 + 0·657 = 11·165.)

Exercise 4·3

Never. It will get closer and closer to zero without actually reaching it because it is a ratio trend curve.

Exercise 4.4

If sales are decreasing by· 6·5 per cent a year, each year's sales will be 93·5 per cent of those for the previous year. Since log 0·935 is $\bar{1}$·971 or − 0·029, the logarithm of the sales in any year will be 0·029 less than that of the logarithms of the sales in the preceding year. The required trend is therefore **− 0·029**, the minus sign showing that it is associated with a progressive *decrease* in sales.

Exercise 4.5

	Additive	Ratio	Difference
January 1961	**250**	**252**	2
February	**240**	**245**	5
March	**230**	**237**	7

The differences between the two sets of figures are small by comparison with the random fluctuations of the original series, and would be unimportant in a short-term forecast. Nevertheless, the differences are increasing with time.

Exercise 4.6

PERIOD				PRODUCTION		
Year	No.	Weight	Components	Value	Logarithm	Logarithm × Weight
1956	1	− 2·5	$p - 2·5t$	6·826	0·8342	− 2·0855
1957	2	− 1·5	$p - 1·5t$	7·125	0·8528	− 1·2792
1958	3	− 0·5	$p - 0·5t$	7·724	0·8878	− 0·4439
1959	4	+ 0·5	$p + 0·5t$	8·245	0·9162	+ 0·4581
1960	5	+ 1·5	$p + 1·5t$	9·324	0·9696	+ 1·4544
1961	6	+ 2·5	$p + 2·5t$	10·004	1·0002	+ 2·5005

Sum of squares of weights: 17·5

Total: 5·4608   + 0·6044

Average: 0·9101

Trend: $t = \dfrac{+0·6044}{17·5} = +0·0345$

Forecast for 1962 = Antilog $(0.9101 + 3.5 \times 0.0345)$
$= $ Antilog $1.0308 = \mathbf{10.730}$
Forecast for 1963 = Antilog $(1.0308 + 0.0345)$
$= $ Antilog $1.0653 = \mathbf{11.620}$

Exercise 4.7

Let $n = $ number of years over which demand doubles.

Then $n = \dfrac{\log 2}{0.0345} = \dfrac{0.3010}{0.0345} = \mathbf{8.7 \text{ years}}$

The statement that demand doubles every ten years is only approximate: the rate of increase appears to be greater.

Exercise 4.8

The log trend t (found from the answer to Exercise 4.6) is $+0.0345$
Antilog $0.0345 = 1.082$
Percentage increase in demand is therefore **8.2**.

Exercise 4.9

True (provided there are no random errors).

Exercise 4.10

True. Only one estimate of the 'trend of the trend' can be obtained, so it *must* be constant.

Exercise 4.11

120 degrees (4 months).

Exercise 4.12

Highest temperature	18°C
Lowest temperature	3°C
Difference	15°C
Amplitude	**7.5°C**

Exercise 5.1

First, in agreeing to co-operate in applying the system and delegating the routine calculations.

Secondly, in collaborating with the production manager to decide the replenishment period from which the re-ordering levels were deduced. (Note that this might also have been done with the aid of a mathematical model.)

Thirdly, in agreeing the risk level on which the buffer stock was based.

Fourthly, perhaps, in refusing to be frightened off by a small backlog (especially disturbing since it occurred during the early months of the new system).

Fifthly, in revising his prediction of sales.

Exercise 5.2

The buffer stock, to cover three months, would be increased to $800 \times 1 \cdot 732 = 1,386$ items. This is 255 more than the two-month buffer stocks on which the ROLs are now based. Accordingly all the ROLs must be increased by 255.

Satisfy yourself that the ROQs are not affected.

Exercise 5.3

$255 \times 4/- = £51$ (see the preceding exercise).

Exercise 6.1

First calculate the increase in the first year:

 500,000 total market − 50,000 current imports (approx.)
 = 450,000 still to be satisfied.
 First year's increase = t
 $450,000 = t(1 + 0 \cdot 9 + (0 \cdot 9)^2 + (0 \cdot 9)^3, \text{ etc.})$

$$= \frac{t}{1 - 0 \cdot 9} = 10t$$

So $t = 45,000$

K

Year	Forecast increase over previous year	Forecast total
(1963)	(base year)	**51,600**
1964	+45,000	**96,600**
1965	+40,500	**137,100**
1966	+36,400	**173,500**
1967	+32,800	**206,300**
1968	+29,500	**235,800**
1969	+26,600	**262,400**
1970	+23,900	**286,300**

The actual figure for 1964 could fit this pair of assumptions about as well as the 200,000/67 per cent pair. Even for 1965, the forecasts do not differ greatly, although both differ greatly from the forecast for unchecked exponential growth, which would be about half a million.

Exercise 6.2

$$\text{Linear Regression Coefficient} = 99,208 - 51,600$$
$$= 47,608$$
$$\text{Forecast for } 1965 = 99,208 + 47,608 = \textbf{146,816}$$
$$\text{Forecast for } 1966 = 146,816 + 47,608 = \textbf{194,424}$$

Exercise 6.3

(a) Nothing: the cumulative sales are well within the action limits and are following the expected trend reasonably well.

(b) Nothing, except to start thinking of some way to stimulate sales, other than a price reduction.

(c) Strict adherence to the control chart would require the sales manager to do nothing yet. However, it seems likely that the line will enter the 'emergency production' area in Week 45 and he may decide to act now.

Exercise A.1

(a) **3**   (b) **6**   (c) **1**

Exercise A.2

(a) $10^5 = \textbf{100,000}$ (b) $10^{12} = \textbf{1,000,000,000,000}$ (c) $10^0 = \textbf{1}$

Exercise A.3

$$\log \quad\quad\quad 1,000 = 3$$
$$\log \quad\quad 1,000,000 = 6$$

$$\log 1,000,000,000 = \mathbf{9}$$

Exercise A.4

$$\log \quad 10,000 = 4$$
$$\log \quad\quad\quad 10 = 1$$

Difference $= 3 = \log \mathbf{1,000}$

Exercise A.5

$$\log \quad 10 = 1$$
$$\log \quad 100 = 2$$
$$\log (10 \div 100) = \log 0{\cdot}1 = -\bar{\mathbf{1}}$$

Exercise A.6

Antilog $10 = \mathbf{10,000,000,000}$

Exercise A.7

$$\log 2{\cdot}154 = \tfrac{1}{3} = \mathbf{0{\cdot}333}$$

Exercise A.8

(*a*) $\log 6{\cdot}813 = \log 3{\cdot}162 + \log 2{\cdot}154$
$$= 0{\cdot}500 + 0{\cdot}333$$
$$= \mathbf{0{\cdot}833}$$
(*b*) $\log 1{\cdot}467 = \log 3{\cdot}162 - \log 2{\cdot}154$
$$= 0{\cdot}500 - 0{\cdot}333$$
$$= \mathbf{0{\cdot}167}$$

Exercise A.9

$0{\cdot}301 = \log 2 - \log 1 = \log (2 \div 1) = \log 2$
$0{\cdot}176 = \log 3 - \log 2 = \log (3 \div 2) = \log 1{\cdot}5$
$0{\cdot}125 = \log 4 - \log 3 = \log (4 \div 3) = \log 1{\cdot}333$
   etc.

Exercise A.10

(a) a number slightly less than 8.

(b) log 5 = 0·699
    log 3 = 0·477
    $\overline{\text{log 15} = \textbf{1·176}}$

(c) True, because 8 × 2 = 4 × 4
    so log 8 + log 2   = 2 × log 4

(d)   log 7 =   0·845
                       log 2 =   0·301
    Difference = log 3·5 =   **0·544**

(e)   log 1 =   0   or log 5 = 0·699
                       log 2 =   0·301   log 10 = 1·000
    Difference = log 0·5 = − **0·301** $\overline{\text{log 0·5} = -\textbf{0·301}}$

(f)   log 3 =   0·477
                       log 100 = 2
    Difference = log 0·03 = − **1·523**

Exercise A.11

(a) **0·7**

(b) $\bar{2}$·000 = − 2, so its antilogarithm is **0·01**

(c) $\bar{2}$·845 = − 2 + 0·845
    = log 0·01 + log 7
    = log (0·01 × 7)
    = log **0·07**

Exercise A.12

(a) **2;   2;   4**

(b) **0·954;   0·954**

(c) log 0·3162 = $\bar{1}$·5
    log 31·62 = 1·5
    To add, take the fractional parts first:
    0·5 + 0·5 = + 1
    Next add the characteristics
    (− 1) + (+ 1) = 0
    Then add the two totals to get + 1 + 0 = + 1
    Antilog + 1 = **10**

Exercise A.13

(a) The characteristic is the logarithm of the next lowest multiple of 10. In this case it is 10 itself, so the characteristic is 1.

(b) **1·0414**
(c) **1·9912**
(d) **2·1761**
(e) **$\bar{1}$·1139**
(f) **$\bar{4}$·0414**
(g) $\bar{4}$·0414+6=2·0414
Antilog=**110**

Exercise A.14

log 12=1·0792
log 14=1·1461
Total: 2·2253
Average=**1·1126** (approximate value of log 13)
log 98   =1·9912
log 100 =2·0000
Total: 3·9912
Average=**1·9956** (approximate value of log 99)

Exercise A.15

Adding log 12 to log 14 gave us log (12 × 14)=log 168. Halving this logarithm gave the logarithm of $\sqrt{168}$, whereas 13 is $\sqrt{169}$. Since $\sqrt{168}$ is **12·96**, this is antilog 1·1126.

Exercise A.16

(a) **0·1875**; **2·1875**
(b) **0·3345**; **$\bar{1}$·3345**
(c) log 2·16=0·3345
   log 2·17=0·3365
   Average=**0·3355**=log 2·165 by linear interpolation.

Exercise A.17

(*a*) **1·63**
(*b*) **1·63**
(*c*) **1,630**
(*d*) Antilog 0·3021 is a number halfway between
2·00 (log 2·00=0·3010) and
2·01 (log 2·01=0·3032).
By linear interpolation we find it to be
2·005.

Exercise A.18

(*a*) Enter tables at row 2·1, column ·05   ·3324
Find entry in column ·004   8
                                                                Add ·3332
                                Add characteristic (0) 0·3332
Our earlier calculation in Exercise A.7 would, if carried to four
decimal places, have given 0·3333, and this is a more accurate answer.
(*b*) **0·0273**
(*c*) **5̄·0000**
(*d*) **5̄·0273**
(*e*) **6·3332**

Exercise A.19

154. (See Exercise A.16(*a*)). The characteristic is 2, so the antilog
lies between 100 (10^2) and 1,000 (10^3).

Exercise A.20

(*a*) **8·752**   (*f*) **0·008492**
(*b*) **2·18**   (*g*) **96·29**
(*c*) **252·7**   (*h*) **1·134**
(*d*) **76·17**   (*k*) **1·208**
(*e*) **30·90**   (*l*) **302,000**

Exercise A.21

302,000

REFERENCES

1 BROWN, R. G. *Statistical Forecasting for Inventory Control*. McGraw-Hill, New York, 1959.

2 BERNERS-LEE, C. M. (ed.) *Models for Decision*, pp. 6–20. E.U.P. London, 1965.

3 ANON. *Case Studies in Production Forecasting, Planning and Control*. American Management Association, New York, 1957.

4 FREUND, J. E. and WILLIAMS, F. J. *Modern Business Statistics*. Pitman, London, 1959.

5 WINTERS, P. R. in *Management Science*, 6, No. 3 (April 1960), p. 324.

6 BATTERSBY, A. *A Guide to Stock Control*. B.I.M./Pitman, London, 1962.

7 WHITTING, I. J. in *Operational Research Quarterly*, 1963, p. 107.

8 ANON. *An Introduction to Business Forecasting*, p. 4. Institute of Cost and Works Accountants, London, 1960.

9 COUTIE, G. A., DAVIES, O. L., HOSSELL, C. H., MILLAR, D. W. G. P. and MORRELL, A. J. H. *Short-Term Forecasting*, p. 14. Oliver & Boyd, Edinburgh, 1964.

10 BATTERSBY, A. *Mathematics in Management*, Ch. 9. Penguin, London, 1966.

11 GREGG, J. V., HOSSELL, C. H. and RICHARDSON, J. T. *Mathematical Trend Curves: An Aid to Forecasting*. Oliver & Boyd, Edinburgh, 1964.

INDEX

Accuracy, 28–9
Additive trend. *See* Linear trend
Aiming-off, 29
Algebraic sum, 21
Alternatives, 3, 4
Amplitude, 72
Analysis of variance, 80
Analytical forecasts, 18–19
Antilogarithms, 105–9
Arithmetic mean, 66
Assumptions, 8–10, 17–18
Automatic forecasting, 13–14
Averaging, 21–2

Balchin, Nigel, 75
Base level, 21, 22
Bias, 29, 43–4
Brown, R. G., 15, 53, 139
Buffer stock, 85

Capitol Records Inc., 16
Causal relationships, 12
Characteristic of logarithm, 107–8
Christmas rush, 97–9
Closed control loop, 17–18
Closing the loop, 17–18
Coefficient, regression. *See* Regression
Common ratio, in exponential weighting, 47
Computer, electronic, 6, 19–20, 75
Confidence limits, 19, 31–2, 67, 93
Control action, charts, and seasonal effects, 89–90, 99
Correlation, 7, 11–12, 16, 75–7
Correlation coefficient, 75
Coutie, G. A., 53
Critical approach to forecasting: introduction, 1; economics of forecasting, 1–2; decisions, 2–4; tactics and strategy, 4–6; question of scale, 6; the critical approach, 6; short-term and long-term forecasts, 6–7
Cycles on semi-log paper, 65

Damping, 52
Data, used for forecasting, 14–15

Decision-making: process of, 1–4; tactical and strategic decisions, 4–5; trends and random fluctuations, 5–6; and question of scale of operations, 6; the critical approach, 6; short- and long-term forecasts, 6–7
Decisions, 1–7, 16; strategic, 4; tactical, 5
Decisions, structure of, 2–4; tactical, 4
Degree-day systems, 74
Dependent variable, 73
Development of a forecast, 7
Deviation, standard, 29–30
Distribution, statistical, 13

Economics of forecasting, 1–2
Effects, seasonal, 10
Errors in forecasts, 1, 12–13
EWMA. *See* Exponentially weighted moving average
Exception, management by, 14
Exponential, definition of the term, 67
Exponential trend, 9
Exponential weighting, 42, 45, 47–8, 49, 67; and secular trends, 52–3; and seasonal trends, 53
Exponentially weighted moving average (EWMA), 48–51
Extrapolation, 58, 62, 65; procedure for 59; to zero, 59–60

Factors, combination of, 3; controllable, 17–18. *See also* Random errors; Rounding off
Forrester, Professor J., 10

Galton, Sir Francis, 56
General Post Office, 7
Geometric mean, 61, 66
Geometrical weighting, 47
Gompertz curve, 97
Growth of sales, 94

Heavy damping, 52
Holt's method, in exponential weighting, 47

Independent variable, 73
Industrial dynamics, 10
Interpolated value, 58
Interpolation, linear, of logarithms, 109–10

Lag, in obtaining data, 41. *See also* Time-lag
Lead-and-lag times, 12
Least squares method, of estimating a trend, 55
Linear interpolation, 109–10
Linear regression coefficient, 56–8, 67
Linear (or additive) trend, 9, 17, 25, 55, 57, 61
Logarithmic regression, 69
Logarithmic transformation, 60–3. *See also* Transformation scales
Logarithms, use of, 60, 103–16
Logistic curve, 96
Long-term forecast, 6–7, 20; case-study of, 99–101
Loop, control, 18

MAA. *See* Moving annual average
Mantissa of logarithms, 107–8
Malthus, T. R., 95
Management by exception, 14
Market, 4–5, 95
Market intelligence, 15
Market saturation, 91; modified exponential trend, 92–3; revising the assumptions, 93–4; growth in nature, 94–5; Pearl's Law, 95–6; Gompertz and other sigmoid curves, 97; the Christmas rush, 97; the sales-proportional scale, 97–9; case-study in long-term forecasting, 99–101
MAT. *See* Moving annual total
Mathematical model, 6, 8
Medium-term forecast, 7
Model, mathematical, 6, 8
Moving annual average (MAA), 23
Moving annual total (MAT), 23; and seasonal effects, 35–6
Moving averages, 21–5; adding, 37;

effect of a secular trend, 25–8; lag versus smoothing, 28–9; precision of a forecast, 29–31; confidence limits, 31–2; estimating secular trends from, 32–5; subtracting moving totals, 35–6; moving annual totals and seasonal effects, 36–7; adding moving averages, 37–8; estimating secular and seasonal trends, 38–41; lag in obtaining data, 41; other aspects, 42
Moving totals, 23; subtracting, 35
Multiple regression, 73–5
Multiplicative trend, 9

Nielsen, A. C., Company, 76–7
Nonsensical weighting, 45

Parabola. *See* Quadratic regression
Pearl's Law, 95–6
Phase difference, 72
Polynomial regression, 70
Population, 12; general theory, 94–5; Malthusian theory, 95; Pearl's Law, 95–6
Precision of a forecast, 28–31
Prediction, R. G. Brown's definition of, 15
Predictors, general, 11
Production capacity, reserve, 1
Proportional growth, 67

Quadratic regression, 68–70

Random errors, 19–22: obey mathematical laws, 13; algebraic sum of, 21; and precision of a forecast, 29–31; and seasonal effects, 83–5
Random fluctuations: trends and, 5–6, 8, 13; and residual error, 13
Ratio constant, 9
Ratio trend, 63
Rectilinear trend. *See* Linear trend
Rectangular weighting, 44–5
Regression, 7, 11, 19

Regression analysis, 12, 19; fitting
straight lines, 54; fitting a trend line
by eye, 56; calculating the slope,
56–8; forecasting by regression,
58–9; extrapolation to zero, 59–60;
logarithmic transformation, 60–3;
forecasting halving or doubling of
present sales, 63; transformation
scales, 64–7; significance of a regression coefficient, 67; quadratic regression, 68–70; polynomial regression,
70; trignometrical regression, 70–1;
vertical and horizontal displacement,
71–2; amplitude, 72; fitting sine
curves, 72–3; multiple regression,
73–5; correlation, 75–7; case study,
77–9
Regression coefficient, significance of,
67
Related figures, 11–12
Re-ordering levels (ROL), 85–6
Residual error, 13
Resources, 4, 7
ROL. See Re-ordering levels
Rounding off, 23–4
Routine, mathematical, 6, 15
Royal Macbee company, 16

Sales, commonly confused with
demand in forecasting, 14
Sales analysis, 81
Sales force, comments of, 15
Sales-proportional scale, 97–9
Scale of operations, 6
Seasonal effects, 10–11; moving annual
totals and seasonal effects, 36–7;
estimating secular and seasonal
trends, 38–41; exponential weighting and, 53; case study in seasonal
forecasting and stock control, 80–1;
sales analysis, 81; sales forecasting,
81–2; random errors, 83–5; buffer
stocks, 85; stock control chart, 86–9;
control action, 89–90
Seasonally-corrected figure, 40
Secular trends, 9–10; adjustment for,

36; effect of, 25–8; estimating, from
moving averages, 32; estimating
secular and seasonal trends, 38–41;
exponential weighting and, 52–3
Semi-log paper, 64–6
Short-term forecast, 4, 6–7, 19
Sigmoid curves, 96, 97
Significant, technical meaning of the
term, 67
Simpson's weighting, 44, 47
Sine curves, 72–3
Sinusoidal regression, 70
Slump, 17
Smoothing, 5, 21–22, 24, 50–1; lag
versus, 28
Sources, emergency, 1
Spectrum of methods of projection, 19
Standard deviation, 29–30
Statistical distribution, 13
Stock control, 1, 80–1
Strategy, 4
Synthetic figures, 15–16
Synthetic forecasts, 18
Systematic returns, 7–8

Tactics, 4–5
Time, span of, 4
Time-lag: in a moving average,
26–7, 32; versus smoothing, 28–9; in
obtaining data, 41; and damping, 52
Time series, 14
Time series analysis, 19
Time-span, of the moving average,
25–7
Transformation scales, 64–7
Trend correction, 29, 32–4
Trend, favourable, 4
Trend line, 55, 56
Trend of a trend, 42, 68–9, 132
Trends: additive, 9; exponential, 9;
linear, 9, 17; ratio, 9 (See also
Secular trends); and random fluctua-
tions, 4–6, 8; secular, 9–10, 25, 32;
seasonal, 10–11. See also Moving
averages; Regression analysis

Triangular weighting, 44, 45–6; table of triangular weights, 46
Trigonometrical regression, 19, 70–3
Two-sigma limit, 31

Uncertainty, dealing with, 12
Uncertainty, three main sources of, 100

Variance, 29; analysis of, 80
Vertical and horizontal displacement, 71–2

Weather forecasts, use of, 11

Weighting, 42; general considerations, 43; types of, 44, 45; rectangular, 44–5; triangular, 45–6; Simpson's, 47; exponential, 42, 47–8, 49; exponentially weighted moving average, 48–51; exponential weighting and secular trends, 52–3; exponential weighting and seasonal trends, 53; exponential weighting compared with triangular, 51
Weights, 43
Whitting, I. J., 99, 100
Winters, P. R., 53
Working forecasts, 16